A White Minority in Post–Civil Rights Mississippi

Thomas Adams Upchurch

Hamilton Books
an imprint of
University Press of America,® Inc.
Lanham · Boulder · New York · Toronto · Oxford

Copyright © 2005 by
Hamilton Books
4501 Forbes Boulevard
Suite 200
Lanham, Maryland 20706
UPA Acquisitions Department (301) 459-3366

PO Box 317
Oxford
OX2 9RU, UK

British Library Cataloging in Publication Information Available

Library of Congress Control Number: 2004108860

ISBN 978-0-7618-2962-1

To Linda

CONTENTS

PREFACE

WHY THIS STORY SHOULD BE TOLD

Black-white race relations has traditionally been the most troubling domestic issue the United States has had to face. Nothing else has been quite as divisive and potentially explosive an issue, year after year, generation after generation. American political and religious leaders fought over slavery as far back as Colonial times. The Founding Fathers argued over it in writing the Declaration of Independence and the Constitution. Congress haggled over it in the Missouri controversy of 1820, the Mexican Cession controversy of 1850, and throughout the abolition movement. Even the destruction of slavery in 1865 did not end America's race problems. Instead, it exacerbated them, as white northerners and southerners, and Democrats and Republicans, bickered over the fate of black Americans in the new order.

Reconstruction brought gains in civil rights for blacks that were won and later lost at a dear price. By the 1880s, the Jim Crow era of segregation, disfranchisement, educational inequality, economic proscription, and racist lynchings had brought more misery upon blacks than slavery ever did, and race relations in America only grew worse thereafter. By the turn of the twentieth century, the color line had been drawn so clearly that white racism and black acceptance of second-class citizenship became socio-political orthodoxy—the equivalent of our modern "political correctness." No one, not even the extremely popular President Theodore Roosevelt, dared question the national zeitgeist by challenging the racial status quo.

Changes in this way of thinking, which kept whites in the position of superiority politically, socially, and economically, came slowly. Decades passed before any notable victories in civil rights occurred. By the end of World War II, the time seemed right, for several reasons, to start the pendulum of public opinion on racial issues swinging back in the opposite direction. Among the reasons for the change were: the publication of Swedish sociologist Gunnar Myrdal's influential book *An American Dilemma* and Melville Herskovitz's almost-as-influential book *The Myth of the Negro Past*; the "great migration" of blacks to cities outside of the South during the war for job opportunities and the resulting birth of a large black middle class; the horror of seeing in Nazi Germany what happens when racism is taken to its extreme or to its logical conclusion; black athletes, such as track star Jesse Owens, world champion boxer Joe Louis, and baseball player extraordinaire Jackie Robinson, excelling at sports invented by white men for white men; black entertainers and writers, such as opera star Marian Anderson, actor Paul Robeson, and novelist Richard Wright, excelling in their fields with white audiences; the advent of the most liberal U. S. Supreme Court in American history beginning in the 1940s, which allowed the NAACP to achieve some incredibly important reversals of earlier rulings and victories in new cases, which began to break down the imaginary color line in various walks of life; and finally, the advent of a Presidential administration–Harry Truman's–which boldly and unapologetically stood in the vanguard of race relation reformers for the first time since the Harrison administration of 1888-1892.

So, in the 1950s and 1960s, the civil rights movement came. Whether white southerners wanted it to or not, whether they were ready for it or not, it came. Like a tidal wave sweeping across a desert plain, it came. It came despite stiff resistance. It came at a great price for some; it came at the ultimate price for others. It was destined to change the face of this great nation, especially its most conservative section, the South, forever.

I was born in the midst of this great cultural convulsion, this tremendous social revolution. And I grew through my formative years when the movement was expiring and giving way to the new world it had created. I am a prototype of the post-civil rights white southerner. I am a first-generation product of the integrated public schools of the Deep South, integrated public facilities, and integrated thinking. For good or ill, that's who I am.

*   *   *

It seems blatantly narcissistic for anyone to write their autobiography, and it seems presumptuously vain for the author to think that a serious publisher would want to print it and sell it. Moreover, it seems the very height of arrogance to expect others to read it even willingly much less enthusiastically. So why should anyone bother? Why should I? What does my life story have to offer that everyone else's doesn't? Haven't all people experienced unusual circumstances of one type or another that deserve remembrance in print? Indeed, and it is this commonness with the family of man that provokes me to lay down my story for posterity, for someday future generations might profit from my experiences. It is with premeditated humility that I tell my tale, knowing full well that in no way will my story affect readers so profoundly as any of the great and famous autobiographies have done. I make no pretenses at revealing anything as shocking or heart-wrenching as one would read in, for examples, the *Narrative of Frederick Douglass* or Richard Wright's *Black Boy*. But to contribute something to the common understanding of southern race relations on the order of Melton McLaurin's *Separate Pasts* or Anne Moody's *Coming of Age in Mississippi* is my goal.

This narrative of my life intends only to show one individual's struggles with the complex racial issues that loomed large in the Deep South in the 1970s, 1980s, and beyond. It is the true story of one boy's growth to manhood, and one young man's attempts to reconcile the ideal with the real. I do not presume to speak for all white southerners of my generation, but my story will no doubt resonate with thousands, if not hundreds of thousands, of them. My literary voice will speak words and thoughts that untold numbers of people surely share silently. Many similar experiences could certainly be found by a mere casual canvassing of whites my age around the Deep South. My story is thus not extraordinary; it is simply a story that has yet to be told and cries out to be heard.

I should point out that this narrative is by no means a complete accounting of my childhood or young adulthood. It is merely one aspect of my life, which, like everyone's life, is quite multi-faceted, containing many sub-plots, such as family matters, romance, athletic endeavors, academic pursuits, day-to-day work routines, and religious practices, to name only a few. I have included only as much detail about such portions of my life as I think necessary to establish a context for the parts dealing with race relations. Thus the brevity of the book. Were I to write a comprehensive account of my life, the book would easily be three or four times as long. But while some readers might find those other portions of my life entertaining, I think it safe to say that they would not find them particularly educational or of much historical merit. Because race relations has always been the bane of the South, the story of a white youth's struggles with racial issues in the post-civil rights years should by contrast prove educational and of historical merit.

    Because it is a true story from beginning to end, I can make no apologies for the words spoken, the thoughts revealed, or the actions taken during my childhood, which are herein recorded. If the reader finds certain aspects of this narrative offensive, insulting, degrading, or demeaning, my only comment is that "real life" is often harsh and ugly to us all, and this is the story of my "real life." To change the words to make them more palatable to the modern psyche would be disingenuous on my part. The only liberty I have taken is withholding the full names of the real people mentioned herein, and identifying them by either their first name, their last name, or their nickname (except for public officials, whose full names are supplied). I do this to protect their privacy. So what I present here ultimately is the good, the bad, the morally nebulous, the intellectually ambiguous, the socially tenebrous; the black, the white, and all the shades of gray in between; in short, the warts and all of growing up a white minority in post-civil rights Mississippi.

Thomas Adams Upchurch,
Statesboro, Georgia
May 2005

CHAPTER I

A GREAT SOCIETY BABY

I, Thomas Adams Upchurch, was born in Lexington, Mississippi, on November 4, 1964. This is significant for a couple of reasons. First, this little patch of earth was one of the real hotbeds of civil rights turmoil in the 1960s, and second, this date marked the symbolic beginning of the Great Society. On November 3, the day before I was born, Lyndon Johnson, the Democrat, defeated Barry Goldwater, the Republican, to continue the presidential administration he had begun a year earlier upon the assassination of John F. Kennedy. Midnight of the 3rd-4th ended the election day, Johnson had won, and around 2 A.M., I was born. I always joke to my history students (in my locally-famous dry wit) that Johnson could not have had his Great Society until I was born. And although I got here as fast as I could, I made him wait two hours for my arrival. Then, of course, I mention under my breath how it turned out that there would not be much "great" about the Great Society. So, perhaps I jinxed Johnson's presidency by my birth!

The small town of Lexington (population about 2,500) is never mentioned in the same breath with the "major" locations of civil rights activity–Greensboro, Little Rock, Birmingham, Selma, Montgomery, Albany, etc.–but it was just as important in its own way. It is infamous in history for hosting the first chapter of the White Citizens' Council ever created after the organization was chartered in nearby Indianola, Mississippi. It gained national notoriety during the movement for the knock-down-drag-out running feud between white female newspaper editor Hazel Brannon Smith, who won the Pulitzer Prize in journalism in 1964, and the local Citizens' Council, which objected to her "moderate" stance on civil rights. It also made national news by driving the Providence farm, a white-black rural cooperative out of business, a story which has been immortalized by civil rights author Will Campbell in a book called *Providence*. Later, the same white power brokers would make sure that the racially moderate Presbyterian Church in Durant ceased services. Later still, Holmes County would be featured in a muckraking *expose* on the popular television news magazine "60 Minutes" as the land that time forgot, showing that the relics of segregation could be found all around Lexington even in the 1980s.

My birthplace is also infamous for being the point of origin of the 1969 United States Supreme Court Case *Alexander v. Holmes County Board of Education*. My state and county held out against enforcing the 1954 *Brown v. Board of Education* ruling as long as anyone in the nation before the *Alexander* ruling hammered the last nail in the coffin of segregated education in America. At about that same time, black Holmes Countian Robert Clark was being sent to represent his district in the Mississippi legislature–the first black to do so since Reconstruction. This story has been immortalized from the vantage point of Melanie Neilson–a wealthy, pampered, white girl who broke racial ranks to go to work for the Clark campaign–in *Even Mississippi*. It is a story not without episodes of violence and intimidation. There are dozens of other less famous but equally disturbing incidents in the civil rights history of Holmes County, including murders, bombings, arsons, and cross-burnings. Indeed, resistance to the civil rights movement was as pronounced in Holmes County and especially its county seat Lexington as it was anywhere in the nation.

I, of course, knew nothing of the turmoil surrounding my birthplace in those early years of my life. Being born right in the midst of the civil rights movement, I never had the opportunity to see the before-and-after snapshots of history that people older than me viewed. I only saw the gradual integration that was taking place through the eyes of a child. I had nothing to compare it to or contrast it with. Kids just a few years older than me bore the brunt of the painful transition. My brother, who was six years older than me, and my sister, who was three years older, both had to endure the awkward, uncomfortable, often ugly integration of the public school system in Mississippi. I remember riding in our big blue Chevrolet Impala station wagon with my mother to pick them up from the Lexington public school before integration kicked in. I recall the feeling of fear and wonder that gripped me as I looked up at the giant building with the huge front steps and thinking, "I'll be going to school here one day." Meanwhile, Momma and I listened to the radio. The song that was playing is still vivid in my mind; it is a song which I love to hear to this day. At the time I had no idea how ironic the words of this song were. Now it is, of course, painfully clear. "I'm no better and neither are you, we are same whatever we do . . . There is a yellow one that won't accept the black one that won't accept the red one that won't accept the white one . . . Different strokes for different folks . . .I'm everyday people. Yes, the song was "Everyday People" by the mostly black sixties band, Sly and the Family Stone.

I never got to go to that school. In fact, that year 1969 proved to be the last year that my brother, sister, or any whites would go to that school. Integration was about to hit, and my family, like so many other poor whites, would be caught in the crossfire between rich whites and activist blacks. I would soon get in on the ground floor of the already-integrated public school system in 1970, in the nearby town of Durant. In that sense, history was kinder to me than to my older siblings, since they had to adjust to this new situation and I did not.

My father, Billy Adams Upchurch, was and still is a good man. He was not nearly as racist as most of his peers, as best as I can tell. He was born in Lexington in 1933, right in the midst of the Great Depression, during Franklin Roosevelt's "Hundred Days" of New Deal legislation. He grew up barely knowing his own father, who was a barber and apparently an alcoholic. My daddy lost his father at an early age, then lost an eye on the playground shortly thereafter. He was the youngest of several children. His older brothers had gone off to fight in the Pacific in World War II and/or Korea after that. Daddy was too young for the world war and couldn't get into the Service for the Korean War because of his glass eye. His mother, Edna Adams Upchurch, raised him, and did a fine job of it, pulling the family through the depression and the war years. My grandmother Edna had been the first person in my immediate family to go to college. She graduated from Berry College in Rome, Georgia, during the World War I era, making her a member of the first coeducational graduating class in that school's history.

Daddy lived in that same house where he was born, on a corner lot of Cemetery Street (so named because it dead-ended at the town cemetery about a half-mile from our house) with my grandmother and eventually my mother and all of us kids, too, until 1969. The neighborhood was a poor, cramped, working class area. The Upchurch house was a small white wood-frame home, with a gravel driveway and ditches on three sides of the yard, a hedge row on one side, and roads on two sides. The yard was probably a quarter-acre, but it, like the house, seemed much larger to me as a child.

Within a couple-hundred yards in any direction from our house, there was a black neighborhood. I remember seeing black children, but never playing with them. I don't know if someone taught me to fear going into the black neighborhood or if I just instinctively was afraid of the unknown. What I do remember, however, was learning to ride my first bicycle at about 4 and 5 years old–without the training wheels, of course; they just slowed me down!–and riding it down those streets where the black people lived. I was not, therefore, petrified with fear by any means, although looking back on it, it may have been wiser if I had been. (My great fear at that age was not blacks but a certain German Shepherd that lurked stealthily in the front yard of a white family's house at the end of the road near the cemetery. I remember riding my bike by that house and that big dog chasing me. I was scared witless! Terrified! I feared big dogs thereafter for many years. Eventually, I learned to fear other things instead, such as vampires and UFO's, but that's another story.)

My mother, Rowena Dickerson Upchurch, was raised a farmer's daughter in neighboring Attala County, a red-clay hill county that had fewer big land-owning farmers and more yeomen than Holmes County. She was six years younger than Daddy, and from all the photographs I've seen of her from her 1950s high school yearbooks, she was quite an attractive young lady (and now quite an attractive older lady), and therefore a nice catch for my old man. They married in 1956, and had their first child, my brother Ricky, a year later. Three years or so after that, they added my sister Susan, and three years or so after that, I came along–unplanned and unwelcomed. Yet again, two years later, my younger sister Carroll was born. ("Carroll" was obviously no name for a little sister. So I called her "Dodo." It just sounded right to me. She forever after became Dodo to me and "Dodie" to everyone else.) My mother clearly had her hands full with the four of us. Especially with Susan and me. Ricky and Dodie were both rather passive, easy-going kids, but Susan and I were both aggressive and domineering types. There was severe sibling rivalry in my household, and there were some serious power struggles among us.

My family enjoyed the services of a black maid when I was a toddler. I don't remember her name or her presence in my home. In those days, it was not unusual for white families to hire black maids and nannies. Black women took those jobs because they had few alternatives. It was part and parcel of the pre-civil rights movement society of the South, but it was a tradition that carried over into the 1970s where I come from. A friend of mine still had a black maid/nanny as late as 1975. I remember her. Her name was Bea. She was a sweet lady. I was shocked to find out one day that Bea gave my 12-year old friend his daily bath! This fellow was a big ol' hulk of a redneck boy who was heading into puberty and this old black lady was bathing him every day! (Egad! I thought.)

As a toddler, I loved to accompany my mother to the grocery store. In the late 60's, there was not yet a single franchise store in town. The grocery store was instead a mom-and-pop operation called "Tom's." It was small and cramped. Looking back on it, I don't know how Momma managed to buy enough groceries from a small store like that to feed a large family like ours. Anyway, one day in the store, we saw two very obese black women at the check-out stand. They both looked to weigh in excess of 250 pounds, and they stank so bad that I wanted to vomit. They were coal-black but they had something white on their noses and under their arms. To this day I don't know what it was, but as I recall, someone told me it was mold, like a fungus that was growing on them because they did not take baths. Talk about making an indelible negative impression on my young mind! Common knowledge back then among local whites was that blacks were nasty, filthy, dirty, and stinky by choice. That belief was no doubt responsible, at least in part, for whites not wanting to mix or associate with blacks. The fear that it would "rub off" was not so much a pigment issue, therefore, as a germs, lice, and disease issue. With the wisdom that comes from hindsight, observation, and education, I know now that no more blacks than whites ever "wanted" to be dirty. Some probably HAD to be for lack of running water and indoor plumbing in their houses in rural and town-ghetto Mississippi in the late 60's. But otherwise, perhaps those who did not bathe were mentally ill, and the mentally ill come in all colors! (There was a white family in town that I know for a fact did not bathe because the patriarch believed bathing was unnatural, and of course there was also the possibility that the hippie culture of the sixties was responsible for some people not bathing.)

My childhood in Lexington lasted only five years, so my memories of it are sketchy, and most of them don't involve black-white issues, although a few do. I remember laying in my baby bed looking up at the ceiling in our house, seeing the square tiles with brown water spots on them. That's probably the first memory I have of anything in life. I couldn't have been more than 2 or 3 years old. I remember watching parts of the first Superbowl game on television in 1967 (I developed a love of football while still in diapers). I remember seeing my first snake. It was a green grass snake beside a big tree in our yard. I promptly killed it repeatedly with my big brother's BB gun (which I was not supposed to play with), then ran to the house, yelling for my folks to come look at what a noble thing I'd done! I remember killing a blackbird with the same BB gun, then taking it in the house and asking Momma to make us a blackbird pie, just like in the nursery rhyme she had often read to me. I remember falling out of the back of my Daddy's pickup truck and hitting my head on the gravel in the driveway. I remember sneaking off into the neighbor's garden with my little sister and being enticed by the beautiful red (HOT!) chili peppers, sitting down in the dirt, biting into one, then screaming bloody murder and crying. I remember playing in the road, in the beautiful white fluffy fog of the mosquito truck, never knowing that it was poison, and being completely oblivious to the danger of oncoming traffic. I remember watching "Laugh-In" on t.v., having no clue that it was inappropriate for children— but my parents didn't seem to care if we watched it.

Speaking of my family's t.v. watching habits, as a side-note, we also watched the "Flip Wilson Show" faithfully, which seems to defy the stereotypes of whites in the deep South in the late 1960s. It was Daddy's favorite show. A few years later when "Sanford and Son" and "Good Times" came on the air, we never missed an episode. Again, they were Daddy's favorites. What he didn't like to watch was "All in the Family." He didn't like Archie Bunker's politics, I guess. Those shows which tried to mix politics and humor, we didn't watch.

I remember amazingly a lot from my five years in Lexington to have been so young. I remember making my first friends there–three brothers named Robert, "Runt," and Rex. (Runt's real name was Anthony, but it didn't sound right to me to call him that. I think I heard his mother call him Runt as a one-time term of endearment, but that's all it took; he would forever be Runt to me. When I called him that, everybody else started to as well, and the name stuck for the rest of the poor guy's life!) I remember making my first girlfriend there–Debbie (and what an awesome first girlfriend she was! She was a tomboy, and we had fun, fun, fun! together for about a year). I remember my parents owning a "trailer park" briefly, into which a new family moved. I marched right up to their front doorstep, completely like a grown-up, knocked on the door, and asked the lady who answered, "Do you have a little boy I can play with?" She thought that was the cutest thing, and said in a distinctly British accent that reminded me of "The Monkees" which I watched on t.v. all the time, "Why, of course I do!" Her name was Pauline, she was indeed from England, having married a former Navy officer, and she introduced me to her son Ricky, who was my age. Since I already had a big brother named Ricky, that confused me. I sorted it out by calling my new friend "Little" Ricky, because obviously my brother was "Big" Ricky. The poor boy got labeled "Little Ricky" for the rest of his life, too, despite the fact that he grew up to be quite a large fellow and much bigger than my older brother!

I remember playing all the games that kids play, such as having a competition with my guy friends to see who could urinate the furthest up the tree in my front yard, not realizing or caring that the old couple on the front porch across the street were watching us . . . and such as betting the girls that they couldn't urinate standing up like I could (I was a mischievous little). I remember my parents throwing a cocktail party, while us kids were supposed to stay in the back of the house with the baby sitter. But I, of course, could not do that. I had to sneak into the living room where the grown-ups were, hide behind the couch, and whenever an adult would set down a shot glass or a mixed drink, I'd pick it up and drink it. I got drunk (and very sick!) for the first time at about 4 years old.

I remember playing by the road, where there was a big "horse apple" tree. We kids would pick those horse apples, which were green fruits about the size of a softball, and throw them at things (and sometimes each other). One day while playing out there, a bumble bee got after me. Not knowing any better, I swatted at it, which made it mad. It came at me, I ran, it stung me, and I screamed bloody murder all the way home. I remember camping out in the backyard with my brother and some of his friends, and seeing my first shooting star, which seemed to fall in the pasture across the road from our house. We promptly took the flashlights and headed out across the pasture to check it out, but alas, came back empty-handed.

My last memories of Lexington came in my final summer there, which was 1969. I remember big earth-moving equipment being unloaded into the pasture where the falling star was no doubt still smoldering somewhere under a cow patty. The Caterpillars, dump trucks, and heavy machinery fascinated me. As the construction workers began plying their trade, they piled up huge mounds of dirt where once the cow pasture and fishing pond stood. All of the kids in the neighborhood would gather to play on the giant mounds of fresh, soft, brown soil. One day, we had a dirt-clod fight. I lost. I was playing with boys my brother's age, who felt no compunction about using me as a target. I got tagged in the head with a big ole' clod (it's a wonder I didn't lose an eye), and ran home screaming to Momma.

I never knew what they were doing with those earth movers, never knew what they were building. All I knew was that right after that, my family packed up and moved to Durant, the next town over from Lexington. Turns out that what was going on there in the pasture was the good white businessmen of the Lexington Citizens' Council had decided that they could not win the battle against the integration of the public schools, so they would build a private white academy in town. The world had just turned upside down around me, and I never knew it.

Clearly, the earliest years of my life were not consumed by racial issues, despite the civil rights upheaval surrounding my community. How can a child be oblivious to such incredible happenings, you ask? I don't know for sure. But it may help put things in perspective for me to say truthfully that I also had no knowledge of the ongoing Vietnam War until it was ending and American troops were pulling out of Saigon in the disgraceful evacuation of 1975 that has been immortalized in television news footage. I did not know that the Vietnam war existed, even though it started at about the time I was born. Instead, my little friends and I would "play" World War II in our backyards. That was the war we were familiar with, from watching movies and from listening to grown-ups talk. So it was with the civil rights movement. I never knew it existed until after it was over.

CHAPTER II

DESEGREGATION AND ITS DISCONTENTS

Durant, the town my family moved to when I was 5, was in many ways the mirror image of Lexington in the 1960s and 1970s. The two towns had kept a rather fierce rivalry going for decades, especially in high school sporting events, when the game of the year would always be the Lexington Yellow Jackets versus the Durant Tigers. The ratio of blacks to whites in Durant was about 70-30 back then; today it's more like 80-20. Quite a few other poor white families moved into Durant around 1969 and 1970 for the same reason that mine did. When the public schools were forced to integrate, many went from being totally white one year to totally black the next. So, not surprisingly, many white families with means preferred to remove their children and place them in the new academies that were springing up all over the state. There were no less than 4(!) academies operating concurrently in my small county, which, when figured according to the ratio of schools to white families, was the highest of any county in the United States (which speaks volumes about the degree of racism extant in my little part of the world).

Poor white families like mine would have done the same in most cases if they could have come up with the money. Some poor families mortgaged their homes, sold their land, disposed of one vehicle or any other worldly possessions they could realistically part with, and anything else they could possibly figure out to do, in order to avoid the "shame" and "degradation" of sending their kids to school with the "niggers." But alas, poor whites did not factor into the equation of the Citizens' Council and their well-to-do members and allies. This was not just a white man's world I lived in, it was a well-to-do white man's world; poor whites be damned! I didn't know the reason for our moving. All I knew was that it was very exciting to me as a 5-year old. If a move is unavoidable, the best possible age for it is pre-school. I didn't have the adjustment problems that my older siblings had. I made new friends and took to my new surroundings easily. Besides, we had not moved half-way around the world, but just to the next town over, which was approximately twelve miles away. My family had lots of kinfolks in and around Durant, too (all of whom were on my mother's side), and that was nice. The fact that I had never attended any school before also made it easy for me to make the transition.

The transition was extremely difficult for Daddy, considering he had never lived anywhere else before (except for a brief stint in Houston, Texas, when he was a young man looking for adventure, which he recalled with dread and loathing as an experience that was anything but a great adventure). There were other reasons for his discomfort, though. His mother died that same year. That by itself depressed him, needless to say, but the implications of that loss were great. She had provided free child-care for us toddlers, and she had helped pay the bills. Without her, my mother would either have to do all the child-raising or get a job. Either way, the family suffered. Add to that the freakish new burden of paying private school tuition for four children, and the depression was made four times worse for Daddy. His choices were few and unpleasant. He decided the best way out of the predicament was to sell the family home and land, move to Durant, which was the only town within a fifty-mile radius that would have a "decent" integrated public school (meaning one which would have a preponderance of white administrators and teachers, if not students) and try to make the best of it.

There was, of course, the natural fear of the unknown in his mind about sending his kids to a school with blacks. What would it be like? Would his kids and the other white kids, being badly outnumbered, be bullied or beaten by the black kids? Would he have to worry every day about his daughters being sexually teased, taunted, or . . . worse . . . by black boys? Would his daughters make friends *too well* with the black boys? All of these questions were considerations, but financially his hands were tied, and there was no other choice.

I don't know if Daddy was just ready for a change of pace in his life or what, but he chose at the same time to quit his job of many years at the Chevrolet dealership in Lexington, where he was the manager of the Parts Department, and take a job at a factory in Durant that made plastics. The factory job paid slightly better, and it was closer to home, but I'm sure there must have been other personal considerations that came into play in his decision. He also eventually gave up his part-time job of mowing the lawns of the Mississippi Power and Light Company's transformer booster stations, which had kept all of us kids busy on summer weekends as long as I could remember. When he quit that job, he made sure the power company hired a black mechanic friend of his named James from the Chevrolet dealership as his replacement. After getting him that job, Daddy called on James occasionally for help with auto repairs, including mine. (We also used another black mechanic in Durant named Calvin, whose shop was in the worst part of town, and whose son was in the same grade with me and was often picked on by other black kids because of how poor his family was. Calvin once had all of his tools stolen from his shop, just at the time that I needed him to work on my little brown '78 Chevy Monza).

That first year in Durant, Momma took me to the school to check me into the first grade. We got there, and the teacher, who looked as old as Methuselah, with her wrinkled, sun-damaged skin, glared at me skeptically, sized me up, tried to talk to me, and saw that I hid behind my Momma and seemed very shy. I was a small child, being from a family which is diminutive on both sides, and due to the combination of my petiteness and shyness, the teacher suggested that Momma hold me back a year. I was happy about that decision. I would not turn 6 years old until November, so I would have been younger and smaller than most of the kids in that first grade class. I was placed in pre-school for one year and got to enter the first grade just before turning 7 years old. This made me a few months older than most of the kids in my class, but since I was small, it didn't seem to matter. And, as it turned out, I was in many ways a very immature child, too (which I can see clearly now but wouldn't have agreed with at the time), which also made the decision to hold me back a wise one.

I have some vivid memories of my entrance into pre-school and first grade. I remember that there were many black kids and not so many white kids, but most of the teachers were white. I never felt out of place in those early years. Being oblivious to racial issues as children are at that age, none of us–black or white–saw anything strange or unusual about being in school together. It seemed perfectly natural to us. I made friends with several of those black kids. One, I remember well, was a black girl named Rosetta. I have no idea who started this or why, but someone began teasing me about Rosetta being my girlfriend. Little boys usually don't like to be teased about having a girlfriend of ANY color or race, so, not surprisingly, I refused to accept the accusation and gave vehement protest. Besides, if I DID have a girlfriend, I confided to myself, it wouldn't be Rosetta, but Sheila, the prettiest little girl in my class, who just happened to be white.

When I started school, my brother Ricky was already in the seventh grade. He was just getting to that age when girls and racial issues hit his radar screen. He had many interests growing up–sports, hunting, fishing, martial arts, motorcycles, music, and making money by mowing lawns, just to name the most memorable ones. No matter what he was into at any given time, I, the little brother, had to tag along and do it, too. He no doubt hated my tagging along, but alas, he was instructed to take me along anyway. When he got into music, it was the new FM rock radio station out of Jackson that he listened to. They played a lot of Led Zeppelin, Beatles, and Rolling Stones type music, and Ricky got into all of those bands and their imitators. He listened to some black artists, too, such as Sly and Family Stone, and Jimi Hendrix. He hung around with some friends who were bad influences on him, but he somehow managed to stay away from drugs, which everybody called "dope" back then. (Daddy laid down the law about that, warning us kids to leave that "damned dope" alone, and it worked for three out of the four of us.) One of Ricky's friends, a white guy named Eddie, got involved in dope and eventually died from an overdose of something; I don't remember which particular drug. Another one of his friends, a fellow named Burrell, got married at a young age to a girl whose family, the Humphreys, had moved to Mississippi from Chicago during the civil rights movement. The matriarch of the Humphrey family was a bleeding heart liberal who taught all of her daughters not to be racists, but to embrace the black race. Well, they all embraced the black race all right. Soon enough, Burrell's young wife had run off with a black guy, and eventually the whole family of women and girls–and it was five of them–started a prostitution ring in town that catered especially to black men. (I witnessed one of the girls making a business transaction in school with a black classmate, which, as you can imagine, made an indelible impression on my young mind, and I later worked with one black guy who told me all about his business dealings with Burrell's ex-wife.)

Anyway, by the time I was in the third grade, Ricky had bought the live double-record album called "Around the World with Three Dog Night." I remember opening up the album cover and seeing the band members' pictures. To me, that was the most glamorous and fascinating thing that I could imagine in my little mind. Rock stars were the ultimate in cool! That particular band, Three Dog Night, had all white members except for the drummer, who was black. He had the most awesome set of gold-rimmed, transparent plexiglass drums of all time!

At nine years old, in the third grade, I began formulating plans to have my own rock band like that. I picked out certain members of my class who I thought were cool, thinking "he'd make a good guitar player," and "he'd make a good singer," etc. Well, there was one black guy in the class, Roy, whom I liked a lot, who was clearly the coolest guy in the class (remember him because he will become quite important later in the story), and, wouldn't you know it–he just happened to resemble the drummer for Three Dog Night. Perfect! He'd be my drummer. I told Roy that he had just been recruited, and he quite naturally laughed. He didn't take my idea seriously and, of course, shouldn't have.

This rock band fantasy started off as just a typical childhood imagination-run-wild type of alternate reality. I also nurtured another fantasy in which I would grow up to be a professional athlete–first a football running back, who would break every record of Jim Brown and the rest of the stars of that late-sixties/early-seventies era–then a baseball player like Willie Mays or Mickey Mantle. My imaginary sports persona dominated inside my brain until I got into junior high school and actually began playing football. Then I was awakened to the fact that what you don't see on t.v. is all the hours of grueling practice that those athletes put in to make their stellar performances; all the heat, sweat, and exhaustion that they endure; and all the bumps, lumps, bruises, cuts, and gashes that they live with every day. So, in junior high, I began to make the transition from my sports persona to my rock star persona. The baseball player persona lingered a couple of years longer than the football persona, however, because I actually enjoyed practicing and playing baseball, whereas in football I only enjoyed the games, and then only when I got to play running back. I did NOT enjoy playing defense. I was actually quite a good running back. I had moves. (My black "drummer" Roy was the star of the team, though, playing quarterback.) Baseball was a kinder, gentler sport to play, but besides that, where I grew up I was a local star at the sport because the level of competition was significantly reduced by the fact that blacks were not allowed to play. Whereas football was a public school sport in Durant, baseball was not. Baseball was a summer sport which was sponsored by the local all-white Lion's Club. So, that limited it to about 30 percent of the population and undoubtedly diluted the talent pool considerably.

Growing up in Durant was strange, now that I look back on it. At the time, I never knew how weird or "backward" my culture was, but it is clear to me now. We went to school with blacks, but we were not supposed to play with them outside of school. We played football and basketball with them in school, but we were not supposed to play baseball with them. We white kids routinely crossed paths with black kids around town, but we always knew that we couldn't play with them the same way. With the occasional exception of a black kid being dared into a "rasslin'" match with one of us white kids, or vice-versa, there was very little physical contact between us outside of school.

Back to the first grade now . . . I do not remember my parents giving me any special advice for dealing with black people as I started school. What I remember is that they (and all white people where I am from) always referred to blacks as "niggers." It was not necessarily a term of derision where I'm from. It might be, but not always. It was a synonym for blacks, coloreds, or Afro-Americans. The current popular term "African American" was not used back then. When whites wanted to speak about blacks who were "decent" or "respectable" or "good," they would call them "Nigras." This term, although generally offensive to African Americans today, was nothing more than the word "Negro," which was always politically correct before the 1990s, pronounced with a southern accent, and it was quite common where I come from. It's the way the white people talked about the black people at church or in front of the preacher. They were clearly careful to be on their P's and Q's, you see. Political correctness of a sort existed even then, and even in Mississippi in a primitive form.

My only teachers in the first two grades of school were white, so I suppose my folks did not deem it necessary to give me special instructions. Beginning third grade, however, that changed. There, I had a black teacher named Mrs. Derrick. She was just as sweet as she could be. She treated all of us children, black and white alike, as though we were her favorite students. And I went out of my way to be teacher's pet with her. She gave us an assignment one time to plant a seed in some soil in a styrofoam cup, then we'd set it in the window of the classroom and watch it grow from day to day. She asked who could get a seed for a garden vegetable from their home to plant, and I, of course, volunteered enthusiastically. I had no clue what I was doing, needless to say, so I went home, found a bag of dried black-eyed peas in the cupboard, put it in some topsoil-less clay out of my backyard and proudly took it to school. Within a few days, sure enough, a plant started to grow, and the class was excited about it. Mysteriously, it never grew into a pea vine and never yielded any peas. I don't think Mrs. Derrick wanted to disappoint me by telling me that it was actually a weed growing in my styrofoam cup. She let me go on in ignorant bliss, thinking I was a future farmer of America.

When a certain family member heard that my third grade home room teacher would be a black woman, I received some special instructions. I was told to be respectful in her class but otherwise not to treat her the same as a white woman. Specifically, I was told, "If she asks you a question, don't say 'yes ma'am' or 'no ma'am;' just say 'yes' or 'no'." Now, as you can imagine, that's pretty heavy duty stuff for a nine-year old to try to digest. I wasn't sure about whether the advice sounded right or not, but it came from someone I trusted and looked up to, so I didn't question it . (Unless you count the perfunctory "why?" that I always asked anytime anyone in authority told me what to do.) As fate would have it, Mrs. Derrick turned out to be one of my all-time favorite teachers, far more worthy of being called "ma'am" than some white teachers I would later have.

Mrs. Derrick made learning fun. Mrs. Derrick, looking back on it, may have had a racial agenda for us kids, however, of which we were totally ignorant. The two things I best remember learning about in her class were both geographic topics. She taught us about this great, grand place called Africa. We learned about the Sahara and the Congo and Egypt and everything else over there. We drew maps of it. I was fascinated with it. It never dawned on me that she may have been teaching us about the dark continent when children in most other schools would have been learning about lily-white European civilization. The other thing she taught us was about a white family named the Kings, who moved out to the middle of nowhere in Arizona sometime in the 1940s or 1950s I presume, and started a town. We learned about all the Indians of the Southwest, such as the Pueblo and the Navaho, which somehow had something to do with the Kings being able to survive in the desert until they got their town established. This was multi-culturalism being introduced innocuously to us southern white kids at an age when we couldn't possibly have known to resist it! Daddy never made a big deal about it, though, I suppose because he knew Mrs. Derrick was my favorite teacher.

My first two years of school had been fairly easy. I had encountered no major problems with classmates yet. Third grade would change that, though. There I encountered my first school bully. His name was Johnny-Wade. He was about a foot taller than me, probably two years older than me, and he was black. He had medium-brown skin and nappy, unkempt hair. He seemed dirty to me. He was the archetypal bully that all of us have had to face with fear and trembling at one time or another. In my case, he would just be the first one that made me quake in my boots, not the last. He and I were not in the same home room, so we did not technically know one another. That, of course, does not matter to a bully. He quickly finds out who the kids are on the playground whom he can pick on. I was one of the unlucky ones. One day on the playground, he accosted me. I have no idea why or what for. I have no recollection of that. The part I remember was when he made an insulting comment to me, I responded in kind, and he threatened to beat me up while pushing me down. I cried and ran to the teacher in charge on the playground. Her name was Mrs. Henderson, and she didn't know me, because she taught fourth grade. She was a black woman, and she was not nearly as nice and sweet as Mrs. Derrick. She was more of a no-nonsense drill sergeant type. She said something to the effect of, "hush all that blubberin' boy and tell me what's the matter." That just made it worse for me. I resolved that I could not count on her to defend my rights against the bully after that.

The next time that Johnny-Wade bothered me, it started the same way, but this time he came charging at me full speed from about twenty feet away. I acted in self-defense, by sheer reflex, with no planning and no thought. When he got right up on me, I turned my head, closed my eyes, gritted my teeth, and just lunged with my hands for anything I could grab. By luck of the draw, I grabbed his brown leather belt, the end of which dangled from his pants about six or eight inches. The belt was clearly a hand-me-down (he was from a very poor family), and it was no telling how old. When I clutched it, it broke off in my hands, and his green corduroy pants hit the ground. There he stood for what seemed like an eternity, but was no more than two or three seconds in retrospect, stunned by the unlikely turn of events. He was unsure what to do, and the whole school yard full of kids was laughing and pointing. He must have felt awful, but for that brief moment, I was on top of the world! There he stood, reaching for his pants down around his ankles, with his white boxers shining in the autumn sun, and I with the remnants of his belt in my hand. Oh, glorious moment!

Unlike in fictional stories and movies and t.v. shows, that embarrassing incident did not stop the bully from harassing me. It just made him more determined to get revenge. I don't recall any other particular events in our ongoing feud, but it lasted for the whole third grade and fourth grade. I passed him going into the fifth grade, I think, while he lagged behind in the fourth for yet another year. After that, I don't remember seeing him again until I was grown. I walked into a Mr. Quick convenience store (our local version of a 7-11), and there he stood. For a split second, I felt fear and panic come over me, but then I decided I should go on about my business. I nodded and spoke to him and he returned both gestures. Life had taken its toll on the big bully. He was no longer that much bigger than me, and he had no doubt been struck down by the reality of his miserable, degraded, wretched, poverty-stricken life.

Heading into the fourth grade, my school problems seemed compounded when I found out that one of my teachers would be Mrs. Henderson. She was a math teacher, and I didn't like math. I wouldn't have liked math even if the kindest, sweetest teacher in the world taught it, and this was by no means a kind, sweet woman. I remember sitting in math class one day while she was teaching us long division using an overhead projector. She turned the lights off in the room to make the projection show up better. I used that as an opportunity not to do my math but to doodle instead. I was sitting there, daydreaming about God-only-knows-what, drawing a picture on my forearm with a blue ink pen. She sneaked up behind my desk, slapped me across my arm and hollered "Boy! Put that ink pen down!" I immediately sank down, tears welled up in my eyes, and wanted desperately to dissolve slowly and sink into the cracks in the floor, but alas, I could not.

I was one of those very (overly) sensitive types. This incident with Mrs. Henderson was not the first time I had cried in school, and it would certainly not be the last, unfortunately. In the third grade, I had had a mean white English teacher named Mrs. Vaughan, who was actually kin to me, for home room. She had laid down the law at the beginning of the school year that none of us kids was allowed even to *ask* to use the bathroom much less expect to actually get permission to *go* during class, because we were under explicit instructions to go during recess. Well, I, of course, was much too busy doing more important things during recess, and one day during English class, I had to GO! No, I mean I had to GOOOO! It was an emergency, yet I dared not ask. I feared this woman like she was the grim reaper. To make the problem far, far worse, my greatest fear was realized when she sent me to the blackboard to spell out words that she called out orally. I stood there at the blackboard with my legs crossed. I winced in pain. I made facial gestures that would have impressed Jim Carrey. I twisted my body such that any contortionist would have been amazed. Finally, when I could stand it no longer, I just let it fly! The resulting yellow puddle filled me with both relief and embarrassment (and filled my shoes with squishy warm liquid!). Somehow, maybe the teacher wouldn't notice, I thought. Maybe I could just escape somehow. Whatever I was thinking, needless to say, it did not work. She, however, was kind enough not to humiliate me further in class. Instead, she asked her teacher's aid to take me home so I could change my clothes.

In fifth grade, I had an equally embarrassing episode, although for a totally different reason. The only thing the two events had in common was that they both involved bodily fluids. I sat front row-center in Mrs. Jones's English class. Mrs. Jones was a no-nonsense white lady, with a reputation for toughness and unfriendliness. She also laid down the law about not asking to go to the bathroom in her class. I was scared of her, and that was not good, because on this particular day, I had a cold and really needed to go blow my nose, but I dared not ask. Right in the middle of our daily class reading, I sneezed. It is fortunate that I covered my face with my hand, because I pulled down a giant wad of slimy green you-know-what in my hand, which was still connected to my nose at the other end. Turns out I didn't have to ask if I could go to the bathroom. Mrs. Jones, giving one of those "that's-the-most-disgusting-thing-I've-ever-seen,-and-I've-seen-a-lot-of-disgusting-things-after-teaching-fifth-grade-students-for-twenty-years!" looks and ushered me to the bathroom promptly. The damage had been done, however. The other kids in class had seen it, and I was utterly humiliated, as you can imagine.

I heard tales of other kids in school who had worse accidents than that just from fear of their teachers or their coaches, or maybe just out of fear to use the public restroom in junior high or high school. They were no doubt mortified by the thought of what thugs might be hanging out in there or who might walk in on them while in the act. (I know I was!) Apparently, one poor white boy in seventh grade, while riding the school bus on his way to a junior high football game soiled himself for fear of asking the coach to stop the bus. The humiliation of that event was so bad, as you can imagine, that his family actually had to pack up and move out of town. For the obvious reason, I will not divulge this boy's name.

Nor was that the only event of its kind that I ever heard of in Durant. Rumor had it that another new kid in school, a white guy who was a nerd and who had just moved to town, had a similar problem. The other kids picked on him relentlessly. A couple of the more sinister white boys–the tough ones who were the locker room alpha males–took advantage of an opportunity during football practice one day to begin the slow ruination of his life. While he was still on the field, they went into the locker room early, emptied out his golden-colored Johnson's Baby Shampoo bottle, urinated in the bottle until it was full, and got the whole football team to gather round and watch as this unlucky and unsuspecting kid later showered and poured the bubbly yellow liquid all over his head. Locker room hysterics erupted. Soon after that, at recess one day, that same sad sack, who was of average height but scrawny, got into a pushing and shoving contest with a skinny black guy in his class. He supposed, as most of us would have, that pushing and shoving would lead to nothing but more pushing and shoving, or, as often happened, a stare down. But Not so. The black guy, whose name was Donnelle but everyone called "Boomer," swung and tagged the white kid in the jaw, and down he went. As he hit the ground with a bloody thud, Donnelle jumped on him and kept beating him mercilessly. None of the white kids came to his rescue, partly because we were all scared and partly because no one liked the guy in the first place. (Ironically, that kid later joined the Marines and put in many years of distinguished service to his country.)

I remember having mixed and confusing feelings about such incidents. I felt instinctively like the thirty percent of students at my school who were white should stick together in defense against any aggression from the seventy percent who were black. I could easily think such noble, daring thoughts while daydreaming or philosophizing with others. But invariably, when the actual time came, I always chickened out.

The other memorable case where a white guy was getting beat up and I did nothing was in the case of Everitt. Everitt was a huge but gangly and uncoordinated kid whom the other kids called appropriately "Mount Everitt." He had suffered through a rough childhood, living in what was essentially a run-down shack out in the woods, with no parents who claimed him, but a grandmother (or was it an aunt?) who raised him. At the time, I never knew how poor his family was or exactly what his personal circumstances were. I just knew that he had come to my church occasionally with his cousin and my good friend Donnie while we were growing up, and I considered him a semi-friend. He had recently transferred into Durant High School from a rural county school a few miles away. He had little in common with us cosmopolitan (note the sarcasm) townfolk. Most of the kids in school found him irritating, including me, once I got to know him outside of church. No one really liked him, and some of the black guys naturally singled him out of the crowd for his size as a white guy whom they could pick on to prove their manliness. One day, while walking down the hall, a whole gang of black guys jumped Everitt without provocation. A white friend named Greg was walking with me at the other end of the hall and saw the whole thing happen. At least five or six blacks wrestled Everitt to the ground and beat on him. My friend Greg and I dropped our books and balled our fists, and thought seriously about intervening, but then we didn't. We just stood there feeling scared and stupid.

After it was over, a few days later Everitt came back to school, and I felt compelled to talk to him. I wanted to apologize for not helping. I was in denial about being scared. I tried to rationalize reasons for not helping, and I don't remember now what reasons I came up with. It doesn't matter. I apologized. To my great relief, he answered "It's ok, I had it coming." Then he proceeded to tell me what a prick he had been and how he deserved that beating. I wasn't sure if I agreed with *his* rationalization at the time, but I'm very sure now that I don't agree with it. At the time, his explanation salved my conscience, but the truth is, I was just plain chicken. That's all there was to it. But I couldn't admit that to myself back then, I guess because I wanted desperately to be one of those alpha males. I saw myself as being one, even though I clearly was not. I think everyone could see that except me.

As a rule, my fears and phobias regarding alpha males were associated with blacks, not whites. Way back around the third or fourth grade, I first heard a name mentioned that sent spine-tingling dread throughout the white community: Walter White, who was actually black, but a light-skinned shade of black. He was a grade or two ahead of me, so I had not yet met him and didn't know who he was, but the white boys in my neighborhood were scared of him. These boys I hung around with were not wimps, either. They were rough and tumble types, yet they shook in their boots at the mere mention of Walter White's name. Naturally, I was terrified. I had nightmares about this character whom I had never seen before. One day, I was playing in my front yard, in the little rental house my family lived in on Highway 51 (the main drag in those days running from Chicago to New Orleans), when I saw a gang of big black fellows strutting across the road toward me. Fear gripped me, but I tried to be cool. As they sauntered across the busy highway, I could hear one of them calling "Walter, Walter." Instinctively, my eyes fixed upon the biggest guy in the pack, whom I then noticed the other boys revolving around as their leader. Could that be the terrible Walter White, I wondered? When they finally got to my side of the road, we all did that thing that kids always do when sizing each other up and checking each other out. We stared at each other suspiciously, nodded our heads, and said something to the effect of "Whussup." The big black boy then asked me my name, I told him, and he seemed satisfied. He was not mean or hateful to me. God! How relieved I was when he and his gang walked on by. After that, I was never scared of Walter White again.

I think it was at that point in my young life that I started to roll the idea around in my head that maybe black people were not that much different from me and white people. Maybe if I just acted nice (and cool), they would leave me alone. Maybe they were like snakes, I thought, if you don't mess with them, they won't bite you. I liked the thought of that. Life would now be much easier . . . so I thought.

CHAPTER III

INTEGRATION AND DIS*INTEGRATION*

It is difficult to remember exactly how old I was or what grade I was in for some of the stories I have to tell. Somewhere in or near the fourth or fifth grade, I saw the transformation of some of my black classmates from being previously friendly to me and other whites to suddenly aggressive and spiteful. One can only assume that as they grew in age and experience, they started to understand the race problem they had been born into, whether through being taught it or just soaking it in through osmosis. With me, it was both teaching and osmosis that made me aware of it, but as I recall it, my awareness of the problem came mainly in the form of reaction to the changes I saw in my black classmates rather than any proactive choice on my part.

The first incident in this transformation came when an ebony-skinned boy named Johnnie went from being one of my better friends in third grade to one of my feared bullies in fourth grade. We had played on the playground at recess all through the third grade. I didn't see him as black; he was just a friend. Over the summer between those two grades, however, he changed. Beginning fourthgrade, he seemed obnoxious. He was bigger than me, but he had never been aggressive before, so I wasn't scared of him. One day, he laid into a fellow white boy in our class named Chip with a verbal harangue and by shoving him. Chip was a shy, quiet, wimpy sort of guy. Since I saw myself as a he-man (a false self-perception that I would hold onto until I was about 30-years old), I decided to come to his rescue. I reprimanded Johnnie, something along the lines of "Hey, don't do that!" I was sitting at my desk and he was standing right in front of me when I said that. He scowled at me and said "Whachoo gonna do about it, Upchurch?" With those words, my righteous indignation caught flame for the first time, and I planned to jump up from my desk and stand up to him. But when I tried to rise, he, standing over me, simply pushed me back down. This response caught me completely by surprise. Not knowing what to do, I naturally tried to get up again. I raised half-way up from my seat, and he shoved me back down. He continued to taunt me, "Whachoo gonna do, boy?" (In our southern dialect, the word "boy" came out sounding like a two-syllable "b-wah," which made it sound far more insulting than the regular English "boy" could ever sound.) I got mad, of course, and tried to rise a third time, and he just shoved me back down. "You ain't gonna do s_ _ _, white boy," he said with a smirk.

Indeed, he was right. I wasn't going to do anything, because I didn't know what to do. My head was spinning with thoughts of replies and reactions that I could possibly attempt, but discretion became the better part of valor, I suppose, and I just sat there, looking at him in astonishment. Mainly, I was confused by his pointing out the fact that I was a "white boy." I hadn't thought much if anything about skin color as a badge of inferiority before that. Suddenly, I began thinking about it a lot. Were white boys not as tough as black boys? Were we less manly? Were we mismatched with black boys in physical tests of strength and fighting ability? These questions started gradually to swirl in my mind, and would over the next few years take on an acuteness that made it seem as if I were obsessed with the desire to prove my manliness and defend the white race from accusations of physical inferiority.

In the meantime, however, I witnessed the transformation of another friend. His name was Berry. He was a chubby, light-skinned black classmate with big, bushy hair. We played chase on the playground, played with marbles and Matchbox cars, and all kinds of other childhood games. I looked forward to playing with him. He was more fun to play with than many of my white friends. But, as with Johnnie, over the summer between grades, a change had occurred. He came back to school the next year very stand-offish and unfriendly. I saw him out in town one day cussin' and smokin' a cigarette. Could this be my friend, who just a couple of months prior had been one of my favorite playmates? Now he wouldn't give me the time of day, and I was confused by that.

Something similar occurred with Robert, another ebony-skinned classmate. If ever there was a wallflower, regardless of race, it was Robert. From first through fourth grades, he had sat in the back of the class completely, totally, and utterly quiet. He may have even been catatonic in his early years. He was small, skinny, and seemed dirty. He was clearly from an extremely poor family. I remember feeling sorry for him . . . until when, in about the fifth or sixth grade, he finally spoke. Out of the absolute blue, he rose up in class one day and unleashed a string of obscenities and invectives against some white girl in class (I don't remember which one). Everyone, and I mean EVERYONE, turned and stared, mouths wide-open, eyes as big as saucers. Robert??? we all thought in unison. Where did THAT come from? Had he just been sitting there all these years stewing on his hatred for white people? Had he just been storing it up? I remember speaking to Robert once or twice after that in the coming years, and he responded to me in a nasty, rude tone. So, I just left him alone. (Several years later, I thought it strange but cool that I picked up the Sunday Jackson *Clarion-Ledger* newspaper, the largest paper in the state of Mississippi, and there was Robert on the front page, a student sleeping on a park bench at one of the state's more prestigious and expensive Liberal Arts colleges.)

Then there was a black girl named Doloris. I had always liked her since first grade. She and I were friends, at least as much as a white guy and a black girl could be friends under the circumstances. (And that wasn't much, let me assure you. A very respected family member once cautioned my siblings and me over the family dinner table one evening: "None of you kids had better ever bring home a black boyfriend or girlfriend," and it would be a law set in stone in my mind from then on. Not that I would have brought home a black girlfriend in the first place, because I never felt attracted to any black girls that way. But there was a girl in my class named Betty who was always semi-attractive to me, and a girl in the grade ahead of me named Katrina was probably the only black girl I ever had anything resembling a crush on. Most black girls were more like Alma, though, to me and all the white guys. Alma was pitch black, skinny as Olive Oil, and very poor and dirty looking. All the guys of both races picked on her and made fun of her throughout grade school. There was a white girl named Wanda whom we treated the same way, also for being poor and dirty-looking.) When I had a terrible motorcycle wreck in third grade, Doloris expressed genuine concern for my recovery, and even cried the first time she saw me all banged up. But at some point in a later school year, she changed, just like Johnnie, Berry, and Robert. She became rude, obnoxious, and in my mind "black." It mystified me. It also made me angry to see these former friends change for the worse.

These were all minor changes compared to what was about to come. Fifth and sixth grades would be the years when my little southern

world turned upside down.   Let me make the disclaimer that it wasn't
ALL bad. I remember some good times from those years, too.
Unfortunately, none of them involved being friends with blacks. I did
have a good black teacher during those years, though. Her name was
Mrs. Jackson. She was an older lady who taught science. She was sweet
and kind to all the kids, and she seemed to make no distinctions between
black and white. In her class, I first got interested in science. I remember
making a "mole machine" model for a class demonstration designed to
show how mankind might be able to "journey to the center of the earth"
one day. She showered me with praise for the good job I did on that
project, and it made me feel like a million bucks. On another occasion,
I made a model of a silicon atom out of pennies glued to cardboard, which
she also highly praised for its creativity. The crowning achievement of
the school year, however, was the science fair. I built an enzyme-making
project, which I took directly out of the back of the textbook. I had no
idea what I was doing, but I followed the instructions and, apparently, I
produced some kind of chemical reaction that made enzymes.

    Mrs. Jackson sponsored the fifth and sixth graders, but she was
not in charge of the fair. Miss Coleman, a hefty young black lady with an
afro and an attitude, who taught junior high science, was in charge. So,
I, along with a white friend named Jackie, had to go to the other side of
the school to meet Miss Coleman and discuss our projects with her. Now,
as you can imagine, just walking across campus to the junior high and
high school side was like crossing over into a whole new world, and I was
scared to death.   Miss Coleman was not the same kind of person as Mrs.
Jackson or Mrs. Derrick, or even Mrs. Henderson.   She was a feisty
product of the civil rights movement. She saw everything in terms of
black and white. She saw a conspiracy around every corner to deprive the
black teachers of equal pay and opportunities for advancement and black
students of equal treatment, etc., etc. She sized my friend and me up. It
was good that I was with this friend Jackie, because his mother was a
teacher in the junior high with whom Miss Coleman had to work on a
daily basis, and therefore she needed to be civil to us.

    I built my project for several days in the after-school hour in
Miss Coleman's class. She didn't seem to be very nice to me, but I don't
think it was a color thing; I think it was a fifth-grader thing. She brushed
off us little kids like we were just in the way. When it came time for the
science fair, we had to ride the bus (the first time I ever rode a school bus.
The town was so small, the kids either walked to school or their parents
dropped them off, as mine did). We rode all the way across town to the

all-black county school called D. A. C. (short for Durant Attendance Center). This school had been built in the 1950s as an attempted stop-gap measure to forestall or prevent the *Brown v. Board of Education* decision from taking effect. The thought among white lawmakers in Mississippi was, if they gave the blacks a "decent" school of their own, they could then rightly claim to be complying with the "separate but equal" doctrine with which they were supposed to have been complying ever since *Cumming v. Richmond County Board of Education* in 1899. The fallacy of the state legislators' thinking, however, lay in the fact that the *Brown* ruling did away with the notion that "separate but equal" was an acceptable social arrangement. So, it became pointless whether the state's schools had in fact become "equal." Indeed, it seemed to me that the all-black DAC school was a better-looking facility than the mixed-race city school I attended. I never thought about the irony of that at the time.

We held our science fair in the gymnasium. The judging was quick, although the waiting before and after the judging consumed most of the day. In the afternoon, the award ceremony was held. They called out the winners in the lowest class first–my class, fifth grade. I was sitting high up in the bleachers with my school group, as far away from the stage as possible, and we were all cutting up and not even paying attention. As they started the ceremony, the Master of Ceremonies said "And the winner of First Prize in the fifth and sixth grade category, goes to Tommie (they always got my name wrong) Upchurch." I wasn't even listening, but I thought I heard my name out of the corner of my ear, and I did a double-take. Huh? My school group started goading me, saying "Go get your ribbon, go get your ribbon." I wasn't sure what to do or where to go, but I got up and started walking down the bleachers toward the stage. It seemed like it took days for me to get there. I felt the eyes of several hundred people on me, and as I passed by Miss Coleman, I saw a big grin on her face. But it was more a puzzled look, like "who is this kid and what project did he do? Where did he come from?" Her reaction, though, was a satisfied "Ok, ok, you go, boy, you go," so I went. I picked up my blue ribbon and triumphantly returned to my seat and waited impatiently through the anticlimactic remainder of the program. Miss Coleman remembered me after that, which is good and important, because I would have to take chemistry class under her in junior high, and she would be my ninth grade home-room teacher.

Before that, though, I had to defend my ribbon at the state science fair which met that year at Delta State University. I didn't win. Nobody from our school won. Miss Coleman was not a happy chaperone on the long bus ride home that night. I had not eaten all day and felt like my guts were twisting in knots inside. Several students and I begged her to stop at a service station to let us buy a bag of potato chips or something, but she would not. Needless to say, I didn't starve to death, despite the fact that I thought for sure I was going to, and I made it home alive around midnight. The reality was, I had never known genuine hunger before that night. That was the first time that I had ever been deprived of my regular meals, and it was actually quite an eye-opening experience for me. In fact, it was one which I would highly recommend that all the spoiled-rotten youth of America experience at least once in their early lives.

Other memories of fifth and sixth grade that involved blacks were neither so instructive as the "starving time" nor as pleasant as the blue ribbon day. Throughout elementary school, we had had a separate library from the main high school library. In the   fourth grade I had enjoyed reading books there. I read juvenile history books like biographies of Sir Francis Drake, Sir Walter Raleigh, and the great Spanish explorers and conquistadors of the 1500s. I also began reading the award-winning books of children's literature, such as *Onion John, Old Yeller,* and *Sounder.* I began to immerse myself in the make-believe worlds of these characters and stories. Being prone to fantasy anyway, and being a naturally good reader, it is no surprise now that I turned into a writer and a historian, although for many years between elementary school and the decade of my thirties, reading was not high on my priority list.

Part of the reason why reading lost some of its luster to me resulted from an extremely bad ongoing experience I had in the fifth grade with the brand new librarian and reading teacher, Mrs. Williams. She was a bronze-skinned, red-haired, lady in her early twenties, probably straight out of college, with an extremely pretty and cherubic face and a Marilyn Monroe-type voluptuous body. Fifth and sixth grades are about the time in a young boy's life when he starts to become aware of the physical features of the opposite sex. It's the start of the "wonder years." All the boys were excited to have this vibrant, young, attractive lady as our teacher. We stared at her. It only took a few days, however, for her to reveal her true personality to us. She was NOT a nice woman. She turned out, in fact, to be as hateful a teacher as I ever had or ever even heard of. She singled out the white kids for punishment on a regular basis. Kids would be talking in class, or just whispering. Whether black kids had participated or not–and they usually did–she would only punish the white kids. I was not an unusually bad student in terms of behavior, but I was prone to be as talkative as everyone else and follow the mood of the class. So, I was indeed guilty of disruptive behavior from time-to-time, but that only made me normal, not special. Mrs. Williams singled me out one day for talking, when everyone else was also talking. She made me back my chair away from the little round reading tables where we all sat, so she could have uninhibited access to my thigh. She took her ruler and slapped me across the thigh with it several times. I was terrified, angry, and traumatized by the event. It was certainly not the first time I had received corporal punishment in school, and it would not be the last, but it was different. It was the only time when I knew . . . I absolutely KNEW . . . the punishment was wrong, that it didn't fit the crime.

Quite naturally, I told my parents about the incident that evening. Momma wanted to see my leg, so I had to take my pants off. Sure enough, there was a big red whelp, which would soon turn into a big blue bruise, across my thigh. She called Daddy in to look at it. He made me tell him what happened. He got mad as hell! The next day, he held me out of school and took me to see the Principal, who was a big black man named Ramsey. (I had met Mr. Ramsey a year earlier in a "Safety Patrol" meeting. I had asked him whether it was true that he had played pro football for the Los Angeles Rams, as rumor had it. From the minds of babes . . .) Mr. Ramsey was savvy about the delicacy of the black-white issue. So, he listened intently and patiently as Daddy scolded him, Mrs. Williams, and whoever else was responsible. Mr. Ramsey wanted to call in Mrs. Williams for a conference with Daddy, but he told the Principle something to the effect of "No, I don't want to talk to her; I might not be able to avoid saying something I'll regret. So I'm telling you. You're the Principal. This better not happen again or your ass will be staring at a law suit!" Mr. Ramsey, of course, had to see for himself the damage. He, Daddy, and I walked down to the bathroom, where I pulled my pants down and got another inspection. Mr. Ramsey admitted the problem looked real enough. But I don't think he was prepared at that point to take any disciplinary action against Mrs. Williams.

I had to go back to Mrs. Williams's class after that, and God!, talk about awkward and uncomfortable! She gave me the evil eye until it burned a hole all the way down to my soul. She was maaaaaaad. It was clear. Ramsey had said something to her. She knew I had just jeopardized her job and career. She was not nice to ANY white kids after that, not even for a moment. The best thing that could have happened to

me after that was what indeed happened. Another white student lodged
a similar complaint against Mrs. Williams. The student was a close friend
of mine with whom I went to church, and with whose family my family
had a lot of interaction. Her name was Pam. She was an extremely good
student, a straight-A student, in fact, who was about as placid and
pleasant, feminine and ladylike, as any girl I ever saw. I used to stay at
her house after school waiting for my parents to get home from work. I
knew her well. There is no way she was acting up in Mrs. Williams's
class. No way. Yet, she got the ruler across the thigh, leaving a physical
bruise, but more importantly, wounding her sweet, innocent, high
standard-pride. This was the final straw. Mrs. Williams finished out the
school year, but she was not re-hired. It was a great victory for the white
students in Durant Elementary School!

To digress momentarily: a few years later in eighth grade, I
would get another "teacher from hell" (as I saw it at the time). Her name
was Mrs. Montague, and she was white. She was actually kin to me at the
time by marriage. She was the most sour and dour human being I think
I have ever met. She taught math, or at least tried to. She rarely did,
because she kept her radar turned on high all the time for catching
discipline problems. One day, during class, a high-yellow mixed-race
classmate named Pierre–whose father was French and supposedly lived
in Chicago although no one in Durant had ever seen him, which led to a
lot of teasing from fellow blacks about his being a bastard–and I were
telling jokes, and had everybody on our side of the class laughing. I had
told Pierre a true story about my catching a baby catfish in a local creek.
The hook I caught the fish on was longer than the fish itself, and
amazingly the catfish swallowed the hook! That story was unbelievably
funny to us eight graders back then. But Mrs. Montague was not amused.
She singled me out of the whole group of boys who were laughing for a
paddling. I think she picked me particularly because she was holding
something against my family because of some marital discord issue of
which I wasn't aware at the time. I don't know that for a fact, but it
seems the best reason I can come up with to rationalize why she didn't
like me.

But victory in the battle with Mrs. Williams back in fifth grade
did not win the war. Larger battles were ongoing, and even more terrible
ones still loomed. Enter here a charcoal-black, smelly, poor, and
nauseatingly hateful racist classmate named Brian-Keith. All the black
kids called him "Brunk," which was short for Brian-Keith. I had never
seen him before that I recall before fifth grade. He was not a loud-mouth,

like most of the bullies I had known before. He talked in a regular tone, but there was something devilish about him. It was in his facial expressions and his voice. My first encounter with him was during class. As far as I know, I was sitting there minding my own business, and he right across from me in his own desk. Out of nowhere he asked me if I had a sister. I told him I did. He grinned an evil grin. He said, "Her name Susan, ain't it?" I said that's right. He smirked and made the most despicable sexual comment that you can imagine one pre-pubescent boy saying to another about his sister. I won't repeat it. Let me just say that it hit me like a bolt of lightning out of the clear blue sky. I had rarely heard such language, and I had never, ever, heard it used in association with my sister. He just waited for my reaction. I don't remember how I reacted, to tell the truth, on that first occasion. All I know is that he had just picked on me for absolutely no reason, and had done so by hitting me where I was the most vulnerable–in my family.

I was destined (and at the time I thought doomed) to spend the next seven school years in the same class with that guy. All through school, I was scared of him. I never saw him fight, but he was always just slightly bigger than me, and he looked and talked so evil, that I just couldn't overcome my fear of him. On one occasion–and I don't recall what school year it was–he made a similar sexual remark about my mother and my little sister, and I just grabbed him out of reflex. I had his shirt balled up in my hand and my face right up in his, and I threatened him. He was clearly not expecting me to defend myself that way, and he didn't respond with anything other than temporary, stunned silence, then he remarked gravely, "you better take your hands off me before I . . .". I don't remember the rest of the details. I did let go of him, because like a dog chasing a car, I had no idea what to do once I had caught the thing.

Even those sexual depravities were not really the worst of this classmate's behavior. He was the guy who single-handedly made me aware that there was more to skin color than just the color of a person's skin. Color was EVERYTHING. Race and racial issues were ALL THERE WAS. Nothing else mattered. If you were black, your mission in life was to strike back at whites. Your mission was to bully and intimidate whites at every opportunity by any ingenious, diabolical means that your twisted mind could devise. He brought all of this to my attention with all the subtlety of hitting me with an 18-wheeler. The first incident I recall occurred on the first day of school after Muhammad Ali ad defeated one of the many white boxers who had the ill-fate to step into the ring with him. I had watched that fight over the weekend (I forget which white guy got pummeled by Ali in this particular fight), and being young and naive, I had not even noticed that the two guys in the ring were different colors. All I knew was that Ali was the superstar of the boxing world. He got all the attention from the famous t.v. sports announcer Howard Cosell. The other guy was just a stick figure. He was just fresh meat for Ali. As a kid, I idolized Ali just like I idolized all the big name sports figures of the day–with no regard for their color. I was rooting for Ali all the way. It never dawned on me that I was "supposed" to be rooting for the white guy. That next day at school, Brian-Keith launched into one of his diatribes. "Dyou see Muhammad Ali beat dat white guy?" he asked. "Dat white mane was a p_ _ _ _; my momma coulda whupped him! White folk cain't fight. A niggah'll beat a white mane evuh time," and on and on and on he went.

That single event changed my life. I started seeing things in black and white after that. Everyday. All the time. I started rooting for the white guy in any athletic competition just to prove that Brian-Keith was wrong. Just to verify my own manliness. And we had an occasional great white athlete to look to: quarterbacks in the NFL such as Terry Bradshaw, Ken Stabler, Roger Staubach, Fran Tarkenton; most major league baseball players, who were still white back then (unlike today); and then there was Bruce Jenner, the great Decathlon winner in the 1976 Olympic games. The point is, I became very defensive of the white race. Looking back on it, I can easily see how some other white boys who grew up in similar situations as mine could have come to embrace the Ku Klux Klan, the Skinheads, the Neo-Nazis, or similar racist hate-groups. The sheer polarization was so incredibly intense when a greasy, smelly (as I perceived it) jet-black classmate talked about the superiority of blacks to whites!

I must admit that at times the thought of moving to Iowa or somewhere like that to get away from blacks seemed quite appealing, although totally unrealistic. A more practical wish was to transfer to the local private school where several of my white friends had already been enrolled for years. Even that desire would never be fulfilled, though, because my parents simply could not afford it. As a last resort designed to help me cope with the unpleasant situation in which I found myself, I figured that I should try to "understand" where blacks were coming from, to try to see things from their point of view, to try to put myself in their proverbial shoes. And I realized even way back in fifth and sixth grade, that many blacks had an attitude today because their ancestors were once slaves. Strangely, I had no concept of segregation or unequal treatment in recent years being the cause of their discontent; the only thing I could see was that it must be slavery.

I remember on at least one occasion telling my nemesis Brian-Keith that it wasn't my fault that his great, great-grandparents had been slaves, so he should leave me alone now. On another occasion I told him that if he was so unhappy with the situation here in America, why didn't he "move back to Africa!" Yes, out of the mouths of babes come some of the most revealing words. Both of those sayings were common among all of the white folks I grew up around–it wasn't our fault about slavery, and blacks should move "back" to Africa, as if they were not born here but had immigrated here to America voluntarily at some point. As a man looking back on such self-proclaimed "pearls" of childish wisdom, it is easy to see the fallacies in our childish arguments, but at the time, they sure seemed to soothe the pain of the daily verbal assaults from the Brian-Keiths of the world.

Without a doubt the most troublesome, divisive, and scary racial period that happened in my childhood came with the airing of the made-for-t.v. mini-series "Roots." I was in thesixth grade. I watched "Roots," as did just about everybody back then. It was THE major event of the mid-1970s nationwide. It was the first movie of its kind, as well as being the first mini-series ever. There was no cable t.v. yet or satellite t.v., so watching some major show that aired on one of the big three networks was as good as it got. Like everyone else, black and white alike, I was fascinated with the story of Kunta Kinte and the whole "Roots" saga. I watched it carefully. On the day after it first aired, just driving up to the edge of campus, I could feel the tension in the air around Durant public school. It was a palpable feeling, like a foreboding, ominous but indescribable "something." I remember seeing etched on the faces of all the black kids–literally ALL the black kids, even those who had always previously been friendly to whites–a suspicious and vengeful look. I felt scared. But then, that was nothing unusual. As it turned out, there were no fights or out-of-the-ordinary goings-on because of "Roots" except that Brian-Keith used it as a recruiting tool. He took advantage of all the suspicion and ill-will among his fellow blacks to convince a whole group of our classmates that whites should be the enemy from then on. And so it was. We became more polarized than ever after that as we headed into junior high. The innocence was gone. The blacks had discovered an ugly and serious part of their collective history, and whites felt a mixed concoction of remorse for the sins of our fathers and defensiveness for the fact that the slavery stuff had happened two and three hundred years ago and had nothing to do with us today.

Brian-Keith continued to be the black thorn in my side throughout junior high, just as he had been in fifth and sixth grades. There were quite a few days that I literally dreaded down to my bones having to go to school, because I didn't want to have to deal with him again. But it went on, day after day. One day in ninth   grade, he was acting up class (as usual) by "pimpin'" and talkin' "jive" and just generally being his usual obnoxious self. Miss Coleman quietly called him out and said "Brunk, your color is showing." That's right, feisty Miss Coleman, the civil rights activist, told this fellow African American that his "color" was showing! He knew exactly what she meant. More importantly, I knew exactly what she meant. It was a wonderful little moment in my short life. To hear Miss Coleman, of all people, tell Brian-Keith to stop acting so "black" was worth its weight in gold in my young mind.

In the long-run, unfortunately, that incident didn't change Brian-Keith's behavior, and he continued to make my life a living hell daily. It strikes me now in retrospect that children are held captive in their circumstances while growing up. Their captivity can be just as harrowing an ordeal as being locked in jail for 12 years. This is something to consider, I now see, when a child is having a rough time in school or in life. I used to think as a younger adult that since I had managed to survive my 12-year ordeal, other kids can do the same. But now I think if there is any possible way that I can intervene and prevent a child from having to suffer . . . SUFFER . . . through year after year of mental and emotional abuse, I should do so. If that means putting my kid in private school or in a religious school, so be it. I won't sit back and force my kid to go through what I had no choice but to endure.

Of course, not all of my troubles while growing up came from blacks like Brian-Keith. Actually, my very worst nemesis of all was a white guy with straight black hair and dark-tanned skin named Lee. He was always an extremely aggressive, pushy, belligerent type of kid, even back in first and second grade. Something happened to him when I was in the fourth grade, though. I don't know what. He suddenly became a bully. Not just a braggartly, bellicose kid, but a genuine, full-blown bully. His mission in life all of a sudden became to beat up everybody in the school to prove that he was the king of the playground, and in fact the alpha-male of the town. He was the only white guy I ever met who even scared the tough black kids. (He made fun of one tough ebony-colored boy regularly, calling him "Spook" to his face, because the boy was pitch black, and the boy, clearly perturbed, thought better of trying to stop him.) He picked a fight with me on the playground one day at recess, for no apparent reason, and challenged me to meet him at Bain Circle after school. That was one of the two places that kids went for "official" fights. These fights became the talk of the school yard all day. Whoever the combatants were supposed to be didn't matter. All the rest of the kids would go out of their way to be at the designated place after school to see the fight. Naturally, in my anger I accepted the challenge. Then immediately afterward when I calmed back down, I thought "Oh, crap, what did I just do?" Or something to that effect.

The truth was, I was scared out of my wits to fight this boy. He was a couple inches taller than me, about 20 pounds heavier, and he was just plain mean! I agonized all day long over what to do. I agonized and agonized. I thought through all the possible scenarios and what if's. If I went and got beat up, I'd want to kill myself. If I didn't go, I wouldn't get beat up, but then I might still want to kill myself. If I went and won the fight (which with my fantasy-prone mind I could actually visualize), I would be a hero. All the girls would love me, all the guys would respect me, etc., etc. But alas . . . by the end of the day, I had rationalized my way out of the fight. This may have been the first time that I prayed for guidance about something so important as this in my young life, or it may have just been the first time I realized that I could "use" my Christianity to save my butt. I decided what I would do is not go to the fight. Instead, I would go home as usual. Then, if and when I had to explain why I had chickened out, I would say because the Bible says that fighting is wrong, and that I'm supposed to turn the other cheek. How convenient! The truth could set me free! (Or, perhaps the "truth" could chain me to a life of fantasy, rationalizations, and metaphysical bungmung so that I wouldn't have to face the real truth: I was a coward.)

Sure enough, the next day at school, the bully teased me and taunted me. But I stood tall and told him that I was a Christian and my conscience wouldn't allow me to fight him, because God had told me that I should forgive him and invite him to church, which I did. He was taken aback temporarily, but shrugged it off quickly in front of all his friends and toadies. Now, on the one hand, I truly had chickened out of the fight because I was afraid to get beat up in public–and rightly so, Lee would have pummeled me that day because he knew HOW to fight, and I didn't–but on the other hand, I had discovered a wellspring of courage that bubbled up from somewhere inside me in a place that I didn't even know was there. I had acted out a fantasy that I'd played in my mind before about being a "real" Christian, just like the ones I'd read about in the Bible–Paul and Peter and those guys. I had found a type of bravery that seemed more noble than the type of self-serving bravery that comes with fighting. Oh, it was self-serving in its own way, to be sure, but somehow I found it easier to visualize myself being beat up for a "worthy cause" than merely to be beat up because the alpha male wanted to prove his dominance over the weaker males.

So, my life growing up was not a total aberration from what most people experience. We all have to deal with bullies and bullying, no matter whether our nemesis is white or black or something else. The only difference in my mind between Lee and Brian-Keith was that in a weird and perverse way, Lee and I were actually semi-friends on occasions after the fight-that-never-happened because of our associations in playing all-white summer baseball and through our families. (My brother worked for a while for Lee's father, who owned a roofing business, and my mother and Lee's mother were best friends for several years.) But with Brian-Keith, there was never anything but enmity from day one to the last day I saw him. He was black. He was evil. He and I would forever be doomed to separation by the dual walls of race and righteousness, like the light is separated from the darkness.

In the eighth grade, while playing varsity junior high football, the coach during practice one day asked which players wanted to "challenge" other players to a "hitting drill," in which the two players would square off and run into each other full force and fury until one guy fell or the coach blew the whistle. Several of the alpha males challenged their rivals, alleged rivals, or would-be rivals. The challengees, like me, tended to be the smaller, quieter players, who just hoped to escape getting challenged. After about 30 minutes of challenges, it seemed about over, and I was turning to go to the dressing room, when it happened. I heard Brian-Keith say, "One mo' coach. I wanna challenge Tawmee (all the black folks called me "tawmee" as if they couldn't say my name "tahmee" in white-speak). So, the coach stopped me and issued the challenge, "Awright Upchurch, you wanna piece of ol' Keith?" Truthfully, I didn't, but I couldn't say no. Besides, this was not like a fight, where there would be no one to pull him off of me. I trusted that the coach (a white guy) would save me. So, we squared up, the whistle blew, and we laid into each other again and again, grunting the noises of football players in the trenches. After we were both exhausted, the coach called time, and told us to hit the showers. It was over. I had survived. I stood toe-to-toe with the enemy and held my own. I don't recall him ever picking on me again, although I still despised him and couldn't stand the sight of him. I just wasn't scared of him anymore.

To digress for a moment, in a later practice, the white coach asked who wanted to challenge whom, and a high-yellow black boy named Kimes, who I think had Puerto Rican ancestry and definitely had a bad racist attitude, actually challenged the coach himself of all people to a hitting drill. The coach was a big, burly man who had long since gotten fed up with the smack he heard from Kimes in practice everyday, so he accepted. Kimes was in full pads and helmet, the coach was in shorts and a t-shirt with a baseball cap. The two got down in a three-point stance, an assistant coach blew the whistle, and the coach hit Kimes like I've never seen anybody get hit before or since. He actually lifted Kimes's feet off the ground by planting his forearm under his chin. The first body part to touch the ground was Kimes's back. Needless to say, he never challenged the coach again, although it did nothing for his bad attitude toward white kids.

Brian-Keith was responsible for one more unsavory event in my young life. It was twelfth grade. We were both grown 18 year-olds by that time, we were in Mrs. Owens's homeroom, and that was one place you did not want to be when you needed an ally like I did that day. Mrs. Owens was an old, holier-than-thou white First Baptist Church lady who taught typing. She was not nice or kind. She was a drill sergeant type. That day my nemesis made one of those "all white people are [you pick your own pejorative and insert here] and they [you decide what degrading thing and insert here] and black people are [overflow with praise, adoration, while choosing your own effusive string of adjectives to insert here], etc., etc., etc. I don't remember, in other words, what he said specifically, just that he said one of those anti-white harangues that I had been forced to listen to for six years. It made me mad as hell! I slammed my pencil down and responded in kind. Mrs. Owens looked up from over her squared-off bifocals and bellowed at all of us students in general to be quiet. She obviously didn't know who was talking, what they were saying, or the nature of the argument at hand. I decided to get up and go to Mrs. Owens's desk and kindly inform her of the hate speech that was going on, courtesy of my black nemesis. She simply blew me off, something along the lines of "you must have done something to provoke him, blah, blah, blah . . .". That made me twice as mad as I was before. I blurted out in a moment of rage a synonym for "Copulate!" and walked away. She called me back, "What did you say?," she hissed, as she pinned back her ears. "You come with me to see the Principal right now!" And off we went.

The Principal at the time was another black man (Ramsey had long since departed for greener pastures) whose name was Kermit. Now, Kermit was one of those names you just flat did not want to have in 1983. Jim Henson's Muppets were hitting the prime of their glorious career back then, and everyone knew Kermit was a frog. So, you can imagine how school kids got their kicks with this guy's name. But Kermit was still the Principal, and he demanded an explanation for why I had "cursed" Mrs. Owens. I explained that I wasn't cussin' her per se; I was letting out my frustration at what Brian-Keith had said and how Mrs. Owens wouldn't do anything about it. We proceeded into a rather in-depth conversation about the state of race relations at Durant High School, in the town of Durant, and in the world in general, which was interrupted sporadically by a rambling soliloquy from yours truly. Let's just say that Kermit could not fully appreciate my take on the issues in question. He suspended me for three days.

I would have welcomed suspension at any other time, but it just happened to come right in the midst of our regularly-scheduled 6-weeks testing. I had a history test the next day. Prior to that, I had maintained an A in history class, with close to a 100-average. Now, I would likely get a big, fat zero on the exam, which would pull my average down significantly. At that time in my life, I was not very concerned with GPA's and school work, but I did have my pride. I had managed to be in contention for Salutatorian of my graduating class (while putting forth a minimal effort ever since seventh grade), and I couldn't bear to see this possibility flushed down the toilet for this silly, stupid, misunderstanding! I decided that if I just apologized to Mrs. Owens, being the good Christian that she was, she'd have to forgive me. We'd just forget this whole thing ever happened. I came to school the next day and sought her out to apologize. And I really did feel burdened and convicted in my spirit for spitting out an ugly word like that in front of this fine, decent Christian lady. Here she came, walking down the hall. I caught her and walked up to her, head hanging low, and sincerity oozing from my pores. I apologized from the bottom of my heart and promised that it would never happen again. She non-chalantly said "I forgive you," and kept walking. She blew me off again! I couldn't believe it. My mind was whirling. I caught up to her again and said, "As a Christian, I believe that . . .", to which she replied that she forgave me "spiritually," but that I'd still have to be punished "physically," blah, blah, blah.

I remember holding back the urge this time to spit out a synonym for "Copulate!" again. That IS what I felt like saying, but I rationalized that she must be right. I guess I did have to do my time. But then, I thought, maybe I could just get my history teacher, Mrs. Poole, a 30-something white lady who seemed to take inordinately good care of her appearance for her age (whose husband was a football coach at the local community college; she was rumored to have had numerous "amorous" affairs with his black players), to let me take the test when I came back from the suspension. I approached her early in the morning before she even made it into the school. I explained what had happened, how it was all just a terrible misunderstanding, and how she knew what a good history student I was. Surely she would take pity on me. Surely she would want to see me succeed. Surely she wouldn't have the cold-heartedness to give me a zero on a 6-weeks test. Surely . . . but she just blew me off. Yes, her too. She didn't seem the least bit concerned about me. So, there I was, screwed. Screwed royally (to use one of our popular colloquialisms of that day). All because Brian-Keith had to go out of his way to ruin my life in the closing weeks of our 6-year ordeal-of-a- relationship.

Needless to say, I did not make Salutatorian. I wouldn't have made it anyway, but that wasn't the point for me. Rather than graduating third in my class, I graduated eighth, just because of one lousy zero on one report card. The girl who won Salutatorian, a white neighbor named Laura, was more deserving of the honor than I was. The guy who won Valedictorian, well . . . I still say his name with virtual reverence to this day. He was a black fellow named Bernard. Ironically, he was the brother of Donelle (Boomer), the mean, hateful, guy who had beat up that white boy at recess that time. Bernard was a model student, classmate, and citizen. He always took every subject equally seriously, unlike me–I blew off algebra and chemistry just because I didn't like them and didn't think them pertinent to my future. Bernard earned the highest honors in the class, and he did so without any artificial props of affirmative action or preferential treatment. He got the same lessons and assignments as I got. He just excelled academically through wanting to. He subsequently went to the local engineering college at Mississippi State University, where he graduated as a Petroleum Engineer. The last time I saw him, around 1993, roughly ten years after we graduated high school together, he was living in Dallas, Texas, raking in the big bucks. And me? Well,

I was working in a furniture factory in Canton, Mississippi, as an assembler making about $6.50 an hour.

As an interesting historical aside . . . throughout these years of the late 1960s, 1970s, and early 1980s, Daddy worked at Weathersby Chevrolet, a dealership in Lexington, as the Parts Department Manager, and Momma worked at Ferguson Discount Drugstore in Durant as a clerk. One of the salesmen who called on both businesses over the years was Byron de la Beckwith, the notorious klansman who was charged with killing Mississippi's NAACP leader Medgar Evers at his home in Jackson back in 1963. Although Beckwith walked free after two trials with all-white juries who deadlocked in 1964, he was later retried and convicted in 1994 by a jury that was two-thirds black, whereupon he was sent to federal prison for life. This story has been immortalized in the movie "Ghosts of Mississippi." It seems surreal to think that someone with such a scandalous past, especially one involving a murder of historical significance, would just go on with his life afterwards as a small-town salesman. But that was indeed the case.

CHAPTER IV

BLACK, WHITE, AND MANY SHADES OF GRAY

When my family first moved to Durant in 1970, we lived in a rental house in a quiet neighborhood. The house, we soon discovered, had a gigantic wasp nest in the ceiling of one of the bedrooms, which the wasps could access from the outside. We got rid of the wasp nest but also got rid of the house as soon as possible. We moved a few blocks down and onto Highway 51, the main drag through town. It was noisy there. 18-wheelers roared by constantly. There was no Interstate 55 opened through Mississippi yet, and wouldn't be until 1974, by which time, we had moved again. In 1973, my family built a new brick house on the other side of town–what could only be described as on the very edge of the "bad" side of town (actually, Durant had several "bad sides," and my neighborhood was just one of them). My folks bought the 1-acre plot from my Aunt Betty and Uncle "Slim." Betty was my mother's sister, and Slim, well, let's just say his name is very descriptive. They lived right next door and had been using the acre for a horse pasture until they decided to sell it to us.

We kids were all excited, as you can imagine, by the thought of building our own house. It would be bigger than any house we'd ever lived in before, and it would be our first brick house, which was something of a status symbol. My parents chose blonde colored bricks, which were still a little out-of-the-ordinary at that time when most bricks were red. I, at nine years old in 1973, helped in the construction, mainly by getting in the way of the carpenters. My Papaw Dickerson was the lead carpenter, and one of his brothers and several of my cousins also helped. I remember hammering and nailing it seemed like all summer while my cousins had their radio set to the rock station in Jackson that played the latest hits of 1973. "Free Bird" by Lynyrd Skynyrd was the most popular song. It was a good summer.

Moving to the other side of town, I had to make some new friends. Fortunately, there were lots of new friends to be made over there. My first friend there was Jeff, who is still a good friend today. We'd turn on his big brother's stereo, crank up "Free Bird" and Ted Nugent's "Strangle Hold" and other such loud electric guitar opuses, pick up his tennis rackets, and commence playing air guitar for hours on end, much to the consternation of his parents and sometimes the rest of the neighborhood. Jeff's family was wealthy, as Durant wealth went. His father was part owner of the Piggly Wiggly grocery store in town. His family always had nice new stuff and always kept their air conditioner on high during the sweltering Mississippi summers, while mine stuck rotary fans in the windows merely to stir the suffocatingly humid air. Jeff had the luxury of attending the private school, East Holmes Academy, located, ironically, in the town of "West," Mississippi, in the northeastern corner of Holmes County, while I went to the public school less than a mile from our neighborhood.

There were other friends over there as well. Jimmy, the boy whose black family maid gave him a bath at 12-years old. Chris (nicknamed "Smut,") one of the good looking, athletic, "cool" guys in town. The Fowler brothers, who first taught me some of the rudimentaries of sex as we walked home from school together. Chuck, whose mother refused to let him join our local make-believe motorcycle gang "The Wizards of Hell" (in imitation of the Hell's Angels), which we played out on our bicycles. My cousin Johnny, who lived right next door and for whom I felt sorry because he seemed overworked by his father. In other words, he didn't appear to have a childhood like most boys did; he just worked all the time, as I saw it. Then there were girls in the neighborhood; not girls to flirt with but girls to argue with and pick on and compete with for the limited neighborhood play areas. And finally, there was Vernon, the big, ebony-black boy with the semi-Afro who lived next door on the other side.

Indeed, my family had built their new dream home right next door to the black neighborhood. Previously, the horse pasture had served as a sort of buffer zone between the white and black neighborhoods. But the perils of population growth and diminishing lebensraum in town had caught up with Durant by 1973. At the time we built the house, there was actually an elderly black preacher who lived next door. I rarely ever saw him that first year. I don't know if he died or just moved away, but about a year later, his house was again occupied, this time by Vernon and his single mother, who had moved to Durant from someplace else, I know not where, but I vaguely recall that it may have been Buffalo, New York. I guess I was in fourth or fifth grade when Vernon moved in. Since he was not placed in the same home room with me that year, I did not officially meet him until a year later. During that first year, he stayed out of sight and thus out of mind for me. But I knew he was there, just as he knew I was on the other side of the fence.

Once we finally met at school, I tried to break the ice and be friendly. Of course, it was that alpha-male type of friendliness that tends to prevail in the grade school years. It is guarded and suspicious, like you're trying to check out the person in question to see whether you can like them and trust them and be friendly with them or not. It all went well at first. He was friendly enough, I thought. At some point, though, and I don't recall when, the relationship headed south, never to be saved. I think it started with my playing "imaginary" football in my yard. I'd get out in the yard and throw the ball up in the air, kick it to myself, and run back and forth pretending to be eluding tackles, just like the NFL heroes I was emulating. One day, I accidentally threw the ball over into Vernon's yard. I was scared to go get it, but I figured sooner or later I'd have to. So, I mustered my courage and talked myself into just brazenly jumping the fence, retrieving my ball, and jumping back like it was no big deal. So I did. After that, I was not so worried about my ball going over the fence. I knew I could just go get it if I had to, like I did before.

In the course of time, around 1976, the ball did go over the fence again, and as I was about to go get it, I heard the screen door slam on the side of Vernon's little red brick house, and out he came. He picked up my ball and at first seemed like he wanted to keep it or play with it himself. I told him it was mine and he needed to throw it back to me. It never occurred to me to invite him over to play WITH me. That was just something that whites and blacks didn't do in Durant. (Here we were, two guys, one white and one black, the same age, in the same grade in school, living approximately 50 feet away from one another for almost 10 years, and never once did we play together!) He eventually threw the ball back, but not before making me angry and vengeful about the situation.

Later, my white friend Jeff came over and we were throwing the football back and forth to one another. Vernon must have seen us. He came out back with his own football and started throwing it to himself. I think he threw it over the fence on purpose, just to see what we would do. I honestly don't remember what I did at first to cause the inevitable confrontation, except whatever it was, I'm quite sure it was designed to show out in front of my white friend Jeff. Vernon and I exchanged unpleasantries, and in my rage, I hopped on my red-white-and-blue bicentennial bicycle and rode it just as fast as I possibly could straight at Vernon. His eyes got as big as saucers, but he merely stuck his hands out, locked his elbows, and braced himself for the coming collision. To my great amazement and consternation, it was like running into a brick wall. I hit him with the full force that my little 4-foot-10-inch, 80-pound body could hit him. . . and stopped dead in my tracks. Then I flipped over the handlebars onto the ground, which is precisely the opposite of what I had in mind. I was stunned, needless to say, and jumped up as quickly as possible to avoid his retaliation.

At that point, Jeff, who was much larger than me in height and weight–probably 5-foot-4 and 150-pounds–although a year younger than me, jumped into the mix. He said, "Leave my friend alone!" and started boxing Vernon. The two pre-teen titans stood toe-to-toe for the next 30 seconds and exchanged blows and near misses in a classic fisticuffs. In the end, both stopped from exhaustion and just growled at one another while gasping for air. I told Jeff, "Let's just go inside," and we went. Vernon left, and we never had another problem living next door to one another.

Vernon and I did have a problem later, however, at school. In high school, probably around ninth or tenth grade, he and I got into an altercation in the library. I have no idea what it was about. It seems strange that I can remember in vivid detail the fight that occurred in my yard when I was about 12-years old, but can't remember the cause of our fight in high school when I was 15 or 16-years old. Anyway, by this time, I had learned a couple of techniques for fighting that I didn't know when I was younger. I had found out from trial and error that, rather than hitting someone with my fist or hand, I could kick them or kick AT them karate-style, and they would invariably respond by trying to kick back. It was just a reflex that they put no thought into. Then when they would kick back, I would grab their leg, and either hold them hostage bouncing on one foot, or twist their leg and drop them to the ground. I preferred holding them hostage, because that way, I got to watch them squirm longer, see them get humiliated longer, and keep myself in a position of power longer. If I dropped them, I lost my advantage. I used this move with great effect twice in high school. In both cases I was defending myself against not black but white guys who were much bigger than me.

In this fight with Vernon, however, I used the other technique I had learned, which was, when a bully picked a fight with me, I would lash out in rage at him fast and furiously and catch him off-guard. From across a table in the library, I lunged at Vernon, who was wearing a black faux-leather coat with a hood on it. I grabbed the hood and yanked it as hard as I could, until it came down over his head and face. Then I pulled back on it so that his body was leaning over the table and he was helpless. I just held him in that awkward position until everyone in the library could see who was beating whom, then I said "You ain't gonna mess with me no more now are ya? You ain't gonna mess with me no more now are ya?" He finally mumbled "Naw, man," and I let him go.

For every defeat in a fight or bullying contest, I had a victory; for every victory a defeat. I won enough battles to keep my competitive nature alive and well, and I lost enough to keep me humble and constantly scared. The majority of my time was spent not in fighting, however, but in avoiding fights. There was a big, light-skinned black fellow with an afro named Dwight in my seventh and eighth grade home room classes. He had failed a grade, and he was much bigger than me. He was one of those fellows who would be nice to you one minute then suddenly turn on you like a rabid dog the next. He asked me politely at the start of the seventh grade to help him with his English homework, and I did. He was just feeling me out to see what he could persuade me to do for him. He then began asking if he could copy my English homework, since we were, after all, "friends." Sharing homework like that didn't jibe with my morals, so I said no. Then he balled his fist and lunged at me like he was going to hit me. He didn't. He stopped abruptly and started laughing. He put his arm around me and said, "Now you know I ain't gonna hurt my boy," and proceeded to apply verbal pressure, adding, "Now you know I gotcher back, little bro." He was trying to make me feel guilty for not helping him by saying he'd protect me from the bullies. In other words, if I would make a deal with the devil, I'd be spared the hell of being an unprotected little white kid in the mean world of junior high school. I'm ashamed to admit it today, but that idea rationalized its way through my mind quite easily at the time. I took the offer. We continued in that symbiotic relationship for two whole school years.

Meanwhile, in the seventh grade, I tried out for the junior high football team. Trying out at my little Division A school (the smallest division there was/is) consisted of telling the coach you wanted to play and then showing up for the first day of practice. I was on the team by default. I had some athletic skills as previously mentioned, but I was much smaller than most of the other boys, especially those ninth graders who had failed a school year. They were fully three years older than me and literally twice my size. There were two black boys in particular whom I remember fitting this category: Glover and Anderson. To me, they looked like brothers. Both were very dark-skinned, the same height, weight, body type, etc. But they had different personalities. Glover was a more jovial, happy-go-lucky sort. He reminds me now of the "Sambo" slave stereotype who liked to laugh and dance and sing. Anderson was exactly the opposite. He was more serious about proving his masculinity. One day at practice, the whole team was hanging around outside the field house waiting for the coach to come out and blow the whistle to start practice. We were in full pads and helmets. I was standing there talking to Jackie, my fellow small white friend, when out of the blue, Glover and Anderson came up behind us and picked us up. They had us in a bear hug with our feet at least 6-inches off the ground. They dangled us there like rag dolls for about 30 seconds, which seemed like hours at the time. I felt so helpless and humiliated. I wanted to do something, but what? I was caught totally off-guard, I was in the clutches of a guy twice my size, and I knew that if he wanted to, he could squeeze hard enough to suffocate me and my friend. Fortunately, he didn't. Instead, both guys just wanted to prove whom the alpha-males were on the football field and remind us little white boys of whom we needed to be scared. It worked.

I had another unpleasant racial experience in the eighth grade with a black person who was older than me, but this person was a girl. Her name was Sherry. She had a hyphenated last name. The altercation arose over just that: her hyphenated last name. I had signed up for algebra in the eighth grade. This course was filled with black ninth graders, me, and my little white friend Jackie. Jackie and I always did things together, mainly because he had a clue and I didn't, so I largely tagged along with him. He thought we should sign up for algebra a year in advance, so we did. We were sitting in class one day, and somebody asked Sherry why she had two last names. What happened next, I cannot account for. I have no earthly idea why I did what I did. I don't know where it came from, but I blurted out "Because she's black." I think it just came out before I had a chance to think about what I was saying or how it would be received. Needless to say, there were gaping stares from all over the room aimed at me for the next 5 seconds, which again seemed like hours. Immediately, I knew I had committed a major, monumental, uuuuuuugly. faux pas. I wanted to reach out and grab the words and reel them back in, but I couldn't.

Why did I say "Because she's black"? I think because back then, the only people I had ever heard of having more than one last name were indeed black. It just goes to show the lack of cultural diversity I had experienced growing up in Durant. Anyway, my saying that could only have been construed as a racial slur, and I realized that immediately. Sherry scowled at me, then struck back like a rattlesnake, saying something to the effect of, "Who you think you are, talking 'bout me, you ol' bumpy-face white boy? You don't know nothin' 'bout me; you don't know nothin' 'bout my name," and on-and-on. Her exact words escape me now, but the part I remember vividly is her calling me a "bumpy-face white boy," which cut me to the quick, because I was extremely self-conscious about having acne, and I had it pretty bad. (By the time I turned 16, I was what they called back then a "pizza face.") So her words hurt me more than mine had hurt her, and I dreaded going to algebra class from then on for TWO reasons (the other being, of course, because I just hated math).

In that same class, there was a short, stocky black fellow named Fred, who along with another black classmate named Dwayne, presented me and Jackie–the two little token white boys in the class–with a condom each. Apparently, Fred had gotten a whole box of them for free from the school counselor's office. He brought the box, which must have contained a hundred or more of the prophylactics, into class and began distributing them around to all the guys (and girls, too!), with a big grin on his face, as though he was performing some extremely valuable service to us all, which we were supposed to appreciate greatly. He handed me one and made some kind of comment about "I know this ain't gonna fit yo' lil' thang, but you can save it for later." Needless to say, I was caught totally off guard by Fred's actions and words, and simply accepted the "gift" without saying a word. I was embarrassed. Thoughts swirled through my brain at a million miles per hour. "Would this guy Fred actually be able to use all those rubbers?" I asked myself. "Would these other guys? Wow, they must know something I don't . . ." etc., etc.

In tenth grade, one of my pre-school best friends, Charlie, and I were in the high school gymnasium weight room pumping iron. Also in there with us was a short black guy named Willie, who was originally from St. Louis, so he had no southern accent, but otherwise had a great deal in common with Charlie and me. He liked rock music, as opposed to soul (which was in vogue in the black community in those days just like rap or hip-hop is today). He was particularly fond of Ted Nugent, so he and I had a lot to talk about. He was a serious weight lifter. Unlike Charlie and me, a couple of guys who dabbled in body building, Willie ate, drank, and slept body building. He was no taller than me, but his biceps were easily half-again as large as mine. He was a short, extremely muscular, even scary-looking specimen of a teenager. He was one of those guys whose massive neck muscles made it appear that his arms were dragging the ground when he walked.

Willie and I had always gotten along before. That day, I had no reason to think that our relationship would change. We were all pumping iron together in a very small room, and body odor was to be expected from a bunch of sweaty guys. But bad breath was not. Unfortunately, Willie had an unusually rancid case of it that day. He nearly made me hurl when he talked in my direction. Adults realize that there is a condition called chronic halitosis, which I'm sure Willie had, but as a teenager, all I knew was his breath could have made a Komodo Dragon nauseous. I didn't want to say anything to him directly about it, because I was not so completely without social graces as not to know better than that. But I did want somehow to subtly let him know. So, I initiated a make-believe conversation about guys walking around with their flies open, or with a big green blob of something stuck in their teeth, or some disgusting thing hanging out of their noses, and other such things that make people look foolish. (And all of these things had happened to me at one time or another!) Then I got around to bad breath. Willie was playing right along, saying "Oh yeah, man, don't you hate to smell somebody's bad breath? I mean, why don't they brush their teeth or somethin'?" etc., etc. I answered, "You know, sometimes people just don't know that they have bad breath," and just looked at him. "Yeah, man," he said, laughing, "somebody oughta tell 'em."

What I said next defied explanation. I probably said it because there was another white guy in the room, and I wanted to impress him. I said, "You ever notice how bad some black people's breath is?" He laughed for about five seconds, then the light bulb clicked on in his head. I could see his expression change. His countenance shifted from jovial to embarrassed, and then to enraged in that five seconds.

He jumped up from the weight bench, clinched his fists, and barked "Whachoo sayin', man? I got bad breath? Is that whachoo sayin'???" I said silently "Oh crap! This is not at all what I had in mind," etc., etc. But the Rubicon had been crossed. There was no going back. I had dug this hole for myself. I stuttered, "uh, yeah, man." That was the wrong answer. Bad, bad answer. He lurched toward me, while I still had both hands on the barbells, and he grabbed me around the neck in a full-Nelson with his massive biceps. He didn't actually want to choke me (at least I don't think he did), and I'm not sure that he had anything planned after the initial attack. I don't remember what he said; I just remember being very scared. Fortunately, he did not hold me in that position long. It was only seconds, I'm sure, but it seemed much longer. After the incident was over, Willie huffed, puffed, and pouted, and I felt embarrassed and humiliated, but I was also defensive of my actions when talking to my white friend. In the days, weeks, months, and years ahead, Willie and I patched up the incident, both of us forgetting it ever happened. I still liked him after that, and he showed no signs of holding anything against me, either. (Every time I'd seen him thereafter, he was chewing a stick of Wrigley's.)

Throughout my junior high and high school years, I was into music. I liked rock music, specifically what is called "classic rock" today. Bands like Led Zeppelin, Rush, and Kiss were some of my favorites. I had spent the majority of my spare time in those years trying to put together a band with white friends. I played guitar and sang (not well), and I taught a couple of other friends to play bass, guitar, and a little bit of keyboarding. We made some music, some home-made tape recordings, and had some performances, but nothing major. A black guy at school named Charles had a reputation as an outstanding piano and organ player. We eventually agreed to get together and play music, despite the taboo associated with a black guy and a white guy hanging out together outside of school. He brought his electric piano over to my parents' house one evening. We set up under the carport. My daddy was not crazy about the idea, but he didn't say too much. Knowing me, if he had made a big deal about having a black guy come over, I would have rebelled and tried to get together with Charles regularly. As it was, Charles and I did not have any musical skills or tastes in common, so we did not play together again for several years. About a decade later, we would get together to pray and hold church meetings, but we still did not have any musical styles in common, so our friendship was not able to blossom.

In the eleventh grade, I had an unusual honor bestowed upon me. I got elected class Vice-President. That was strange because my class was so overwhelmingly black that no whites ever won any offices. Voting generally followed racial lines, not by training or instruction, but by instinct. That year, however, I made a concerted effort to build a coalition to support me for Vice-President. I knew I couldn't win President because a certain black classmate named Frizell had already sewn up that spot. But, I figured if I could convince all of the white kids in class–all 11 of them–to vote for me, I could win a few black votes by promising to vote for them for something. The strategy actually worked. After the election, I heard several black classmates murmuring and complaining about the fact that a white boy had won. They clearly wanted to monopolize the politics of the class.

I eventually got to the twelfth grade in 1982, and finally escaped the following spring in the Class of '83. It was a proud moment, needless to say. I graduated eighth   in my class of 44 (I dropped four places because of that confounded zero I got in Mrs. Poole's class!). Being eighth in my class was not really all that impressive, considering the fact that I come from an extremely low-performing school system. The Valedictorian was the black guy named Bernard; the Salutatorian, the white girl named Laura. I was one of only four white guys to graduate that year, and one of only eight whites in all.

CHAPTER V

FROM HIGH SCHOOLER TO HOLY ROLLER

I graduated high school in 1983, having successfully negotiated twelve full years of the same peculiar public school. Like so many young people, I did not know what I wanted to do next. One of my white friends, Greg, tried to join the Navy, but was rejected for health reasons. He then ended up working at a factory. Several friends joined the National Guard and went into various occupations. Some headed for a university, either Ole Miss in Oxford, Mississippi State in Starkville, or Delta State in Cleveland. Some eased right into Holmes Junior College, the local community college which was just eight miles down the road in the town of Goodman. I worked the first summer after graduation with my older sister's husband in the cable television business. It was not a permanent arrangement by any means, and I had to decide what to do next. I opted for going to work at a factory about 40 miles south of Durant–Madison Furniture Company in Canton–where Greg worked.

Madison Furniture was an interesting, eye-opening experience. I had previously never had to stand on my feet for eight hours at a time for any reason, much less for the reason of slaving away on an assembly line. The reality of the workplace was difficult to adjust to, but it was also a breath of fresh air after years of being cooped up in a classroom. The racial situation at Madison Furniture looked much the same as the racial situation at Durant High School. About 90% of the workforce was black, but about 90% of the supervisors and managers were white. I was among the 10% of whites in the regular workforce, and my supervisor, Cheek, a guy I liked a lot, was among the 10% of blacks in management. On the one hand, such white workers were treated somewhat "special" by virtue of the fact that the managers wanted so desperately to increase the number of whites in their work environment. But on the other hand, I was in a no-man's land. I didn't naturally fit in with the white bosses or the black workers. It was just like high school all over again, only worse. There were days when I would go to work and not see a single white person all day long! I know that sounds incredible, but it is true. It still had not occurred to me at the time, even though I was 18-years old, that I could make FRIENDS with any of my black cohorts. Yes, we could work together and be labor associates and spend 8 hours a day around each other, but we could not really fraternize outside the workplace like real friends, at least not in my mind (and I suspect that most if not all of them felt the same way from custom and tradition).

First opportunity I got to move on to a better job, I took it. Considering Madison Furniture paid about $4. 60 an hour, moving up was inevitable. I got a job at the best factory in the area, Hunter Engineering Corporation, in my hometown of Durant. My older brother worked there, several old high school buddies worked there, and the black-white ratio was about 50-50. I made about $6.10 an hour, which was pretty decent money in rural Mississippi back in 1984. I stayed at the job for nine months, but I still wasn't happy. I wanted something more, but I didn't know what. For years I had entertained thoughts of becoming a professional musician/singer/songwriter. But I had never been lucky in the music business, and it did not appear that that would change. I had to try to set realistic goals, but that was difficult, since I had no idea what I wanted to do other than play music. So I wandered aimlessly in life for months, before deciding that my salvation lay in becoming extremely religious (pardon the pun). And that's what I did.

Meanwhile, my parents felt increasingly hemmed in by our shrinking neighborhood in Durant, which had always been on the edge of the black part of town but now threatened to become totally black due to white families moving out and selling to blacks. Daddy sold our home to a black physician who was just moving to town from Philadelphia, Pennsylvania. Our family home would prove to be nothing more than this doctor's temporary starter home. He would subsequently build a mansion in the countryside a couple of years later. My parents also found some land in the countryside of neighboring Attala County, right on the Big Black River (which is neither "big" nor "black," and some would say not even a "river.") They hired my Papaw Dickerson as our lead carpenter again. I worked closely with this old master craftsman as he built the new family home, which was, ironically, smaller than the one we had just vacated.

Papaw was born around 1910 (I'm not sure about the exact year), so he had lived through not only the civil rights movement but the nadir of the Jim Crow years. Papaw was an interesting character, and not just to me, but to everybody who ever met him. He was about 5'5" tall and might have weighed 125 pounds soaking wet. He had an extremely dark, reddish-toned complexion. His diminutive stature and his dark skin were no doubt products of his Choctaw Indian genes. (I, unfortunately, inherited the small stature Indian genes but not the good skin-tone Indian genes! I'm white, freckley, and ruddy, rather than tanned and smooth.) Papaw never had any qualms about saying exactly what was on his mind. After negotiating an extremely difficult angle for the molding around one corner of the kitchen in the new house he was building for us, he proclaimed proudly to the world, including two black plumbers Daddy had hired, "Ain't no nigger can make a cut like that, and ain't but a few white men can!" I once saw him in a Durant convenience store, owned by one of his old white buddies named Milton, grab a 6'3", 250 lb. young black fellow named Esau around the neck and try to wrestle him to the ground, saying "Grab his legs, Milton! We'll show this buck nigger who's boss!" It was all for a joke, though, and Esau knew it. He just laughed and played right along. I heard tales of Papaw and some other whites riding through the black neighborhoods on weekend nights getting drunk and throwing bricks at their houses and sticking cherry bombs in their mailboxes just for the hell of it. No, it wasn't to scare the blacks into not voting or anything sinister like that. It was just pure mischievousness, like old frat boys who had never actually grown up. The point of my sharing this story is that, evidently, not every bad deed that southern whites ever committed against blacks was due to a diabolical motive or political conspiracy. Some of it was for misguided fun and games, due in part, no doubt, to lack of anything more entertaining to do in rural Mississippi on a Saturday night.

I subsequently got laid off from Hunter, which naturally put me in one of two places–the unemployment line or a college classroom at Holmes Junior College in Goodman. I chose the latter. I enrolled in music classes, thinking maybe it would give me some contacts in the music business. How naive I was back then! I made good grades, but my heart was not really in my course work because I lacked a vision and a purpose. The second semester, I changed my major to Liberal Arts. That was not exactly an improvement over the music major. The big change came not in the classroom but in my extracurricular activities. Since I had always been religious and spiritual, it was only natural for me to attend some meetings of like-minded folks at college. I joined the Baptist Student Union and the inter-denominational Vespers fellowship. It was at the latter that I met a man who would change the course of my life over the next several years.

The man's name was Matthew. He was not the faculty leader of Vespers; he was only a student. He was about four years older than me, but he may as well have been forty years older. He was that much ahead of me spiritually, and just in understanding life. He was what I might call a "Christian Philosopher," although he certainly would not have accepted the label "philosopher." He had a definite philosophy of life, however. He believed in the Bible literally, and he could quote it backward and forward. But more importantly, he actually seemed to live it, which was something I had never before seen outside of a church building in my life. He was humble, gracious, and kind. He was not argumentative in the least, despite his obvious command of the scriptures and his doctrinaire positions on them. And he was a man with a mission. He only cared about one thing–sharing the Gospel. The most amazing thing about him to me at the time, though, was that he was all that and . . . he was black. I had never even met a WHITE Christian like him, despite having been around hundreds of them in my life, much less a BLACK one. Keep in mind that in those days, whites in some fundamentalist churches still questioned whether blacks even had souls! Some even went beyond merely questioning that proposition; I have heard a couple of white preachers stand behind the pulpit and make the statement ipse dixit that black people have no souls! So the thought of a black man being a "better" Christian than whites was an ipso facto impossibility.

Everyone called him Brother Matthew. He had a sidekick with him at the college named Brother George, who was also black. I rarely saw one without the other. I soon found out that George was a new convert who was being tutored by Brother Matthew in the Christian way of life. My white friend Greg and I began looking forward to Vespers more than any other church meeting we attended regularly, because we wanted to hear Brother Matthew expound the scriptures, and we wanted to see the light that shined from him and George like it shined from no one else we knew.

After we got to know Matthew and George better, we developed a friendship that was close enough that Matthew invited us to visit him in his dorm room for continued fellowship. We accepted the invitation. The first time we arrived on his doorstep, he greeted us with open arms, we went in, sat down, and just listened for three solid hours as Matthew shared the Gospel with us, his life story, and his vision for ministry. We were enthralled. Utterly captivated. We had never heard anyone talk with such authority about the Bible. We were spellbound by his incredible ability to explain things that had always before been mysteries to us. We subsequently went back to his room regularly for in-depth sessions and intensive Bible study and prayer. We even took other white friends with us, trying to turn them on to the holiness way. It made a positive impression on some, like Donnie, a big red-headed fellow who had grown up with me in a Baptist church.

It was clear from the beginning that what we two white guys were doing was considered strange by onlookers of both races. Whispering and rumor mongering had us up there in a black preacher's room being "brainwashed." Later on that year, after we attended an all-black church meeting in nearby Lexington which included several single black females, we were accused of "dating" black girls. For us guys, such calumny came and went like water off a duck's back, but those girls bore the brunt of the criticism. Their families and local blacks gave them a hard time about "dating" white guys. I assure you, however, there was never the slightest physical contact between us. We had a spiritual bond with our black brothers and sisters. Nothing more. But that was enough to set the rumor mill running full speed.

At that time in my life, I was 19 and 20 years old, a very impressionable age. I was ripe for molding and shaping. In that sense I guess I was indeed "brainwashed" by hanging out with Matthew and his crowd. But it was a good type of brainwashing in one way, if not in all ways. In less than a year's time, it broke down all the racial animosity and destroyed all the false stereotypes that I had built up over my years of struggling with being a white minority in post-civil rights Mississippi. I had come to see that black people and white people are not all that different. Yes, we may look different, which we have no control over. Yes, our cultural backgrounds may inevitably make us think, talk, and act differently. But on the inside, we're all the same. We all struggle with good and evil, right and wrong, morality and immorality. We all want to love and be loved, to be accepted by someone or some group. We all want to make a decent living in a noble profession. We all want to live at peace with our fellow man. We all want freedom to make our own choices–mistakes and all–in life.

Greg and I (and sometimes others) began driving from Durant to Hazelhurst, Mississippi, about 100 miles away every Saturday evening for prayer meetings at Matthew's home church, which his older brother Malachi pastored. This continued for about a year or so. Over time, the close fellowship I shared with my black Christian friends inevitably gave way to new circumstances in life. Matthew graduated from college and moved off to get a job. I got married to a local white girl. George got married to one of the black sisters in Lexington. Greg joined a local interdenominational and interracial church and got ordained to preach. The ebb and flow of life separated us. Eventually, over about a five-year span of time, we no longer had enough contact to justify calling ourselves a united group. We all just went our separate ways. But not before touching each others' lives in indelible ways.

After I got married, I quit college and went back to work in the furniture factory in Canton. There I gained a reputation as a radical preacher. I employed the scriptural training I had received from Brother Matthew but, unfortunately, without the gracefulness and tact with which he shared it. I was an ideologue. A doctrinaire. I saw the world not as it was or is, but as it should be according to the Bible. That made me extremely judgmental of everybody and everything. This is important because, keep in mind, I was working in a factory that was about 80-90 percent black. Some of my black coworkers were intrigued by my extreme religiosity. Others were simply put off by it. This latter group naturally attributed my modus operandi/modus vivendi to racism. Why? It was all they knew. Everything could be explained in racial terms, they thought. . . the fact that they were working for horrible wages in an oppressive manual labor job while most of their supervisors were white; the fact that they went home to the crime-ridden ghetto while their white counterparts went home to decent neighborhoods; the fact that they sent their children to the almost all-black public school that was falling apart both physically and academically, while their white counterparts sent their children to private schools; the fact that life had dealt them a hand of seemingly unequal opportunities, while whites seemed to possess all the advantages.

I had the opportunity over the next five years to share the Gospel and to experience Christian fellowship with dozens of my black co-workers. I invited some to my home for continued Bible study and prayer meetings. One was J. T., a short, stocky, medium-brown fellow who was quite a bit older than me. J. T. spoke proudly of being a Deacon in his Missionary Baptist Church, but he cussed like someone who had never stepped foot in a church in his life. I tried to change him. He resisted my advances for a long time, but eventually warmed up to me. We made arrangements for he and his family to drive over to my house and eat supper with us one weekend. My wife and I had already planned the menu, bought the groceries, and cleaned the house for our visitors. On the Friday afternoon of the scheduled weekend visit, I wanted to confirm that J. T. and his family were coming. He laughed and blew me off, as if saying "You didn't really think I was serious about coming to a white man's house for supper, did you?"

On another occasion, a different member of J. T.'s church, an old black man named Ernest, invited me and my white Christian friend Gerald to his church (I think perhaps assuming we wouldn't come), but we went. In fact, Gerald was the guest speaker that day. I just sat in the all-black audience. Some of the members of the congregation welcomed me with open arms, some gave me funny looks or dirty looks, and others just ignored me. (Basically, this was exactly the same experience I had always had at any white church I ever attended!) Ernest was one of at least three good black Christian men that I remember working with at Madison Furniture; the others were both pastors–Brother Handy and Brother James. We shared many hours of good fellowship together on the job. Then there was Brother Craig. He was one of the "brothers" from the Holiness clique of Matthew and Malachi's church. He had fallen on hard times and needed a job, a place to live, and a car. I helped him with all three things. I recommended him for a job at Madison Furniture, let him live with me and my wife until he could get out on his own, and let him borrow a car for about six months.

Occasionally I would try to talk to my unchurched black co-workers about religious things and be rebuffed sharply. One black co-worker named Charles told me point blank, "Mr., you better just leave me alone and min' yo' own bu'ness. I don' wanna hear dat bull_ _ _ _ you be preachin.' You mus' think you da only one knows anything. I's a grown mane. An' I's a grown mane 'fo' you's bone. . ." etc., etc. (Only I cleaned up his language a little bit and made it sound milder than it really was, because he was shouting expletives while poking his finger in my face). Later that year, his wife ran off with another woman (yes, a woman), he lost everything in a divorce, and he suffered some kind a strange, rare illness that laid him up in the hospital for months. I visited him in the hospital. It was amazing how different his reaction was to me then.

Another incident involved two young black guys named Troy and Willie. These guys were both about 19 years old, fresh out of high school (I doubt either had graduated, although I'm not sure about that), both were about 6' 3" or 6'4", and both were what they called back then "players," which was a euphemism for "playboys." Troy was one of those guys of whom I could never tell whether he was serious or playing mind games with me. We had long talks about the Bible on a few occasions, and he seemed quite knowledgeable about it. He clearly had some background in a Protestant church of some kind. But he was also obviously in open rebellion against his Christian upbringing, saying things that connected Jesus with his own genitalia in unrepeatable ways.

Willie, to the contrary, was not amenable to discussing the Bible with me. He got quiet the first time I approached him, as if he was taken aback, and he probably was. He said he was raised a Catholic and had attended a parochial school all his life. Over time, he grew loud and militant about not wanting to hear me or any other fundamentalist or Protestant Christian in the factory talk about our faith out loud. He would cuss and talk dirty and do anything and everything to upset the religious tone we "Bible-thumpers" and "holy rollers" in the place had set. One day around Thanksgiving, his rhetoric became so offensive to me, that I just walked up to him and said, "Brother, if you keep this up, I'm gonna tell you about Jesus." To which, he launched into me with a string of obscenities and invectives the likes of which I have never heard before or since. It was frankly humiliating to me.

Picture a 5'6" white guy looking up at 6'3" black guy and threatening to tell him about Jesus. Then picture the black guy getting right up in the white guy's face, except looking down on him and threatening to kill him. That's the way it was that November day. I had no other interaction with Willie again that year. Over the Christmas holidays, the factory shut down for a week. When I came back to work in the new year, Willie did not show up. To tell the truth, I was glad not to have to see him. But when I found out why he was not there, I nearly fell out. He and a group of his young black friends were riding and drinking. They crashed the blue Firebird that Willie drove head-on into an embankment out in the county. The "Firebird," ironically, caught on "fire." Some of the guys managed to crawl out, but Willie was stuck behind the wheel. They said he burned alive, screaming. Obviously, I wasn't there, and I can't verify those details, but it is unquestionable that he got killed in the crash.

Other episodes of black-white relations in the factory were not nearly so dramatic. A big, hulk of a black man named Julius, whom everyone called "Bucky," regularly asked me for money, because he knew I was a "preacher" and thought I'd be compassionate to him. He was right. I loaned him money, usually in $10 increments. (Ten dollars was a lot of money back then, when I was working for $6.50 an hour.) This arrangement went on for a couple of years before it became apparent that he was using the money to buy liquor, and that he was lying to me about it. I finally told him "no" one day. He got mildly upset, but fortunately for me, he was not a violent type of guy. He just gave me the cold shoulder after that, and went on and barked up somebody else's tree.

Another black co-worker whom everyone called "Red" (for his bright orange hair and yellow skin with freckles) would come and go in spurts of repentance and rebellion. He had fathered six children by three different women, and had a female co-worker pregnant at the time, even though he was only in his mid-20s. I tried to help him and encourage him spiritually, and usually he accepted my efforts. But once, after I found out that he was cheating on his income tax form by counting all those children as dependents when he was not actually supporting them, I asked him about it, with the intention of setting him straight. He told me that "de world 'd be a better place if people just mind they own bu'ness." So I did.

Seeing co-workers, whether black or white, vacillate between repentance and rebellion, was quite common. One big black fellow named David worked closely with me for several months assembling sofas. We talked to one another constantly while we worked. He was shacking up with his girlfriend and felt guilty about it. I preached to him about it and saw him change right before my eyes. Then the weekend came, he went home to his girlfriend, and came back worse off than before. This chain of events repeated itself several times before our working partnership got broken up and we went our separate ways.

A white co-worker named Andy, who was my age and my size, became the target of my ministry for several months. He was cool toward me for a long time, but eventually took up with me gradually, being intrigued by my differentness. He was pre-occupied with black-white, male-female relationships. I think he had it ingrained in his mind somehow that he must have sex with a black girl before he could feel like a "real" man. In his mid-20s, he had had his share of white girls, but never a black girl. He always asked me how I felt about such interracial relationships, and I told him my pat answer that it was fornication whether it was between blacks and whites or just blacks and blacks or whites and whites. The only "proper" relationship for such intimate encounters was marriage. I did not think it was wise or prudent for blacks and whites to intermarry, not because I saw it as sinful or unnatural, but because I knew the problems that such couples would face in society and the double problems their children would face. That was the late 1980s, and that opinion was still certainly axiomatic in Mississippi at the time. Each year and decade that has gone by since then, however, the less this axiom has held true. Now I'm merely ambivalent about interracial marriages. I don't automatically advise against them, but I rightly still fear the repercussions that such unions may have on the couple and their children living in the rural Deep South.

Andy, not surprisingly, was also curious about the black male endowment and black female libido. He had the stereotypes firmly planted in his mind: black men had foot-long schlongs, and black women were all nymphomaniacs. He had heard stories of a white girl in his hometown of Thomastown, Mississippi, who had sex with a local black playboy "legend," and she ended up in the hospital with internal damages. I assured him, that while that individual episode may or may not be true, the stereotypes don't hold true across the board. How did I know? I had played football. I had been in the locker room. I had seen what there was to see. Some black guys had big ones, some did not. Some white guys had big ones, some did not. Enough said! Moving right along . . .

Over the span of five years, work in that factory took its toll on me. My health degenerated. Specifically, I developed severe tendinitis in my right elbow and shoulder from the repetitive motion that is the natural by-product of specialized labor. I searched for another decent-paying job (and by "decent-paying," I meant something above minimum wage) for about two years before I found something. I got a job working in a grocery store in the next town up the road, Pickens. In so doing, I managed to escape my tendinitis problem, but life threw me other curve balls, which proved even more devastating in the long run. Suffice it to say, that I got divorced and had to start over in life at that point. That was 1992.

I look back on my days as a self-described missionary to the ghetto workforce of Madison Furniture in Canton, Mississippi, with mixed feelings. On the one hand, I have no doubt that I left a lasting impression on many of my co-workers. On the other hand, I wonder now whether it was an impression for the better or the worse. Only God knows. Whatever the case, I reached out to the black community intending to do it good, but did so working within my frail human limitations, which now fills me with doubts about the efficacy of my efforts.

I did not stay at the grocery store long, and have no major racial incidents to report there, except to say that I witnessed some of the most appalling cases of poverty and most egregious abuses of the food stamp system there that you can possibly imagine, and almost all of them involved black customers. Pickens is in the southeastern-most corner of Holmes County, and it is the small hub of the countryside extending into three other counties. It is 15 to 20 miles in every direction from Pickens to get to a town of any size where there are jobs and schools and opportunities. Many of the people who live in the countryside are extremely isolated from civilization, making only one trip to town per month, generally right after they get their next installment of food stamps. Often, they traveled communally, meaning several families or parts of several families would all pile up in two or three jalopies and ride to town together. Their old cars, sometimes little Datsuns, Toyotas, Chevrolet Chevettes, or Ford Escorts, would be overflowing with people and their bumpers hugging the pavement when they pulled into the grocery store parking lot. Then, they would proceed to ransack the store for three or four heaping buggy-loads of groceries, which they would pay for with food stamps. Then a poor bag-boy like me would have to take all those groceries out to their cars, and find ingenious ways to vacuum pack them in the trunk, set them in people's laps, and sometimes tie them to the tops of the cars with rope!

I always felt sorry for those families. But there were just as many cases where a nicely-dressed, bejeweled black customer would drive up in a brand new $30,000 Lexus, Acura, Cadillac, or such, then pay for their groceries with food stamps. In some cases, they were buying groceries for their infirm parents or grandparents or neighbors, but in most cases, they were buying them for themselves, and they were simply milking the system because they could. One black entrepreneur in town made his rather lucrative living by giving cash for food stamps, because many of his clientele would prefer to have money for buying liquor or tobacco or gasoline or whatever. I'm not sure exactly what arrangement he had going, whether it was offering 50 cents on the dollar or what, but he had a large enough clientele–I dare say perhaps a hundred regulars–that he made a killing. Shortly after I quit working there, however, this man, whose name I don't recall, was nabbed in a federal sting and sent to prison for his illegal activities. I'm sure that his arrest and incarceration did not make the problem go away, though, for someone else probably stepped into his position and took right up where he left off.

Subsequently, I got a job as a manager of a fast-food restaurant. Again, I didn't stay at the job long. I stayed long enough, however, to learn for a fact that I didn't like working in the restaurant business. The man who hired me for that job was a white guy named Fred. He was a nice, Pentecostal man who was younger than me. He'd been in the franchise for several years–I think he started right out of high school–and had managed to work his way up to district overseer for the franchise. About 3 months into my brief tenure there, something happened, I know not what, and Fred got fired by the regional superintendent. His replacement was a black man named Anthony. Anthony was nice enough at first, and I didn't think anything bad about working for him. But over the space of a couple of months, I began to think he didn't like me, and soon enough I learned for a fact that he had no use for me. Even though I was doing a good job and making a healthy profit for the company, he wanted to get rid of me. My suspicion was that I was one of only two white store managers in his fleet, and he wanted to push me out so he could promote my black assistant manager. I have no proof for this belief, but I am convinced it is the reason he seemed so anxious to get rid of me. I mean, there really was no other reason that I could see. When I tendered my resignation to him, I was hoping he would prove me wrong and realize that he'd been too rough with me and ask me to stay on. But no. He accepted my resignation before I had spit the words out of my mouth completely, and said essentially, "Don't let the door hit you on the way out."

Another job I held very temporarily was as a delivery driver for a telemarketing firm selling coupons for various local businesses. One of my many deliveries was to the girls dormitory at Jackson State University at night. Jackson State was and is a predominantly and traditionally black college in the inner city of Jackson, Mississippi. I was the only white person there, and I felt uncomfortable. I got some ugly stares but no threats. Even so, it was not a place I wanted to go back to, especially not by myself, at night, to the girls dormitory! The black Holiness church group that I fellowshipped with met at another all-black college a few times, Mississippi Valley State University in Itta Bena, but I never felt uncomfortable there, perhaps because I only went on Sundays and to the chapel and was always with a bunch of people.

Although one would expect that the level of civility in race relations would be higher on a college campus, no matter which college or what type of school, such was not always the case. As a student at Delta State University in Cleveland, an integrated college which is about 60 percent white, I was run off the sidewalk deliberately by a group of black athletes walking toward me. I know it was intentional because they took up the whole sidewalk, made no attempt to share it with me, and one of them stuck his elbow out just as I was walking by and hit me. Needless to say, I was quite disturbed by this little incident, but could do nothing about it under the circumstances. Another time walking down the sidewalk in front of a girls dormitory at Delta State, a group of black girls was hanging out a third-story window hollering at passersby. As I came by, one of them yelled, "Hey, you white studmuffin!" I didn't know whether it was a compliment or a sarcastic slur. I ignored it and kept walking.

EPILOGUE

YOU CAN'T GO HOLMES AGAIN

Most people go through a period of rebuilding at some point in their lives. For many, divorce is the reason. For others, it is a catastrophic illness or a natural disaster that causes it. Like so many others, I felt sorry for myself for a long time before shaking it off and getting back on my feet. The process of rebuilding was slow and painful, and often it appeared that progress consisted of taking one step forward and two steps back. Eventually, I determined that my immediate salvation would lie in going back to college. Not knowing what to major in even after all those years in the school of hard knocks, I decided on Social Studies Education, not because I had any driving desire or intense passion for the subject, but because history, civics, and geography had always come natural to me as a student. I thought, therefore, that I might enjoy teaching those subjects. Even though I was now 29 years old, I still had no genuine knowledge of history or any other field of social science. Other than knowing the history of the Bible, Biblical peoples, and Biblical lands, I was almost totally ignorant of history. I would clearly be on a steep learning curve. Once I got into the field, however, and had a clear direction for my future, embracing that learning curve would not be a dread but a delight.

I finished my community college prerequisites in about a year of part-time and full-time study, then I headed off for senior college, where I would live in a dorm and sequester myself for hours on end with my head in a book. To my great relief, history and other social sciences/humanities in general still came easily to me, and making straight A's was not at all out of my reach. Going into history as a discipline is not something that people should do unadvisedly. There are few jobs available with a history degree. Like most history majors, I did not know what field of history I wanted to specialize in, but I would find out by trial and error. Turned out that the field which immediately gripped me and would not let me go was African-American history. Why would a white southern redneck like me be drawn like a moth to a flame by black history, you ask? Because there is no way to study black history without studying the interracial relations of blacks and whites. Therefore, I and my family tree comprise one side of the equation of black history. This is admittedly a convoluted way of looking at the field, but it is not inaccurate. In most instances in American history, the destiny and plight of blacks was determined as much or more by white politicians, owners, overseers, employers, and neighbors as by black leaders such as Frederick Douglass, Booker T. Washington, or Martin Luther King, Jr. It thus seemed (and still seems) perfectly natural to me that I, a poor white southern redneck, should be fascinated with African-American history.

I wrote my master's thesis at Delta State University on a local racial topic. The thesis was entitled "Race Relations in Holmes County, Mississippi: The First Hundred Years, 1833-1933." It was basically a short narrative of the history of my stomping ground from the era of the Peculiar Institution to the beginning of the New Deal (which coincidentally happens to be the time when my Daddy was born). In researching the thesis, I found something that seemed a little bit startling to me. Rather than reading dozens and dozens of accounts of brutality and unfair treatment against blacks, I stumbled across many instances where blacks and whites cooperated for the mutual good. Their relationship, on the whole, appeared far more symbiotic than antagonistic. What historical records don't tell us, we can only infer. And we can certainly infer that Holmes County had its sad share of racial animosity prior to 1933.

Although I have never published a scholarly paper on Holmes County race relations post-1933, I have done quite a bit of research on the topic over the years. What I have found is that there seems to have been a notable turn for the worse in race relations in my little corner of terra firma after the civil rights movement commenced than there ever was before. My research has been somewhat corroborated by testimony of certain whites who lived before, during, and after the movement, as well as by current observation of the conditions of the county. According to these eye-witnesses, blacks and whites lived side-by-side in Lexington in the aforementioned symbiosis prior to the 1960s, notwithstanding the fact that the relationship was clearly one of white dominance and black subordination. Their take on the movement was that it merely served to agitate a group of people who were previously content with their condition. Civil rights activists such as Martin Luther King, Jr., simply convinced local blacks that they "should be" unhappy rather than leading them in a racial revolution because they "were" unhappy. In other words, the movement and its leaders turned the vast majority of contented blacks in the rural South into malcontents. By this reasoning, it would have been better had the civil rights movement never occurred.

Of course, if one keeps in mind that the same basic argument was used by whites to justify and uphold the slave system a century earlier, then this anti-civil rights movement ideology loses some of its luster. As a professional historian, I am bound by the unwritten code of ethics that applies across the board in all fields of research and scholarly inquiry, which requires intellectual honesty and psychological flexibility, admitting when theory and observation do not align, casting off speculative premises when verifiable and empirical data prove them false. Therefore, I cannot accept prima facie the oversimplified version of events that some whites give about race relations being worsened by the civil rights movement. Yet, that does not mean there is no truth at all in that contention, because current observation shows that Holmes County has suffered its worst years economically, if in no other way, since the civil rights movement. The county was a thriving, bustling, growing area of Mississippi until the 1960s, with an abundance of both industrial development and agricultural jobs. But since then, hundreds of white business and industrial leaders, educators, doctors, lawyers, and other professionals, have left the county in a gradual but steady exodus. As they have left, plants have shut down, storefronts have been left vacant, real estate values have plummeted, and now some of the once-upscale parts of Lexington are nothing more than run-down rows of old Victorian mansions. It is a classic microcosm of the "white flight" phenomenon that has been made infamous in America's big cities in the post-World War II era.

Today, as for the past 30-plus years, Holmes County has the dubious distinction of being one of the most economically depressed, educationally lagging, intellectually deprived, and perpetually behind places in the United States. I feel saddened every time I go home to visit my old digs in the heart of Mississippi. What makes me doubly sad is the fact that I have not moved to New York, California, or some other bastion of progressivism; I have not moved to a place that is on the cutting edge of economic opportunities, material abundance, or intellectual stimulation, but merely to semi-rural Georgia. People who are life-long residents of Statesboro, Georgia, find it incredible that this town which they take for granted is so much more prosperous and well off in any number of ways than the place from whence I came. I have friends from the Midwest who have seen dire poverty while driving through some Indian reservations in the Dakotas, and have seen the squalor of inner-city ghettos in Detroit, Chicago, and St. Louis, but they have never seen anything quite like some of the black communities along the dirt roads where I come from, unless they have been to Haiti, the Amazon, Africa, or Indonesia. In other words, it would be difficult to compare some of the areas in and around Holmes County to anything else in the United States; one would have to look to third-world countries to find a close equivalent. Case in point: the New Tribes Mission Institute, a Baptist missionary training school, opened a branch in Holmes County back in the mid-1970s which is still running today. Reason: Holmes County offers racial, cultural, and topographical conditions as comparable to those found in the remote, poverty-stricken, technologically backward hinterlands of the world as can be found anywhere in the United States.

Then there is the race relations problem, which has not gone away since the civil rights movement, but has rather changed forms. In a sense, the roles are now reversed between blacks and whites. The full weight of the black vote has now come to bear on local elections, making it quite difficult for whites to win public offices in the county. Black judges, sheriffs, mayors, city councilmen, and county supervisors now fill posts that 40 years ago were all lily white. Has this role reversal led to a rise in the quality of life for blacks in Holmes County? Only in symbolic terms–of self-esteem and race pride. It has certainly not helped raise the standard of living for blacks there because the loss of white power has resulted in a proportionate loss of economic opportunities, as already mentioned.

The race problem also continues to manifest itself in more sinister ways, such as in crime and the criminal justice system. But again, the roles are reversed now. Think of all the infamous lynchings and racially-motivated white-on-black murders and acts of terrorism in Mississippi before and during the civil rights years. It seems that young black hoodlums are today taking advantage of the black-dominated law enforcement and judiciary of Holmes County just as white thugs once milked the lily-white system to their own benefit. In the mid-1980s, a couple of black teenage boys who had gone to the Durant public school with me broke into a house shared by two white twenty-something women and raped them violently. One of the women was able to identify one of the assailants as a guy named Marvin, whom other kids in school used to pick on for being skinny by calling him, not surprisingly, "Starvin' Marvin." Local law enforcement dropped the ball in this case, however, which caused the white boyfriend of one of the victims to take the law into his own hands, at least symbolically, by burning a cross in the middle of the black part of town where Marvin lived. To my knowledge, justice was never served in this case, although criminals usually become repeat offenders and are eventually nabbed for later crimes, which happened with these rapists.

A much more notorious crime occurred in the mid-1990s, becoming the most sensational news story to hit Holmes County since the Hazel Brannon Smith saga of the early 1960s. There was a tiny white-owned general store called Pinkard's Grocery on the edge of the black part of town in Durant. It had been there as long as I can remember. I had bought many soda pops and candy bars there as a kid. One day around closing time, a black teenage boy entered the store with a heavy metal pipe in hand, and bashed in the skull of the elderly white lady named Mrs. Roberts who was attending the cash register. She, needless to say, died. The black Chief of Police in Durant, who was an honest and sincere man just trying to do his job impartially, suspected it was a certain guy with a record of petty offenses (even though he was only 14-years old!) named Culp, and arrested him. The white District attorney, James Powell, prosecuted the case against the accused. The boy admitted to being in the parking lot of store when the crime occurred, but claimed he saw a white man run from the store and jump into a car and make his getaway. This testimony caused an outcry in the black community that was enormous and unbelievable. A locally-famous black defense attorney named Lumumba jumped into the case on the side of suspect, played the race card, and turned it into a brouhaha. With this legal posturing, and with an all-black jury and a black judge, the attorney managed to get the case against his client dismissed. Loud, prolonged "hurrahs!" went up throughout the black community, as they perceived that justice had been served to their defendant. The outcry in the white community was then equally enormous and unbelievable, although seemingly muffled in the national media due to the out-of-control political correctness of the day.

Considering that this case occurred in the immediate aftermath of the O. J. Simpson trial, the Rodney King trial, and the first set of accusations against Michael Jackson, it is not surprising that political correctness ruled the day. If the crime had been one of a white assailant bashing in the skull of an elderly black lady, I believe Jesse Jackson would have been Johnny-on-the-spot, and it would have been plastered all over the national television news. Be that as it may—or may not be—the boy walked free. About a year later, a white teenage couple from Texas were eloping to Alabama to take advantage of that state's lax marriage laws. They passed through Durant en route to Alabama. While waiting at the bus station, which was located on the edge of another one of the black parts of town, our aforementioned black teenage criminal Culp and an accomplice accosted the teens, put them in their car, drove out into the country to a dirt road, shot the white boy, dumped his body in the ditch, raped and beat mercilessly the white girl (whose name is withheld here intentionally), and left her for dead in the ditch. She did not die, however. She was hospitalized locally for many weeks. She was eventually able to give law enforcement an accurate description of her tormentor, and, sure enough, it was you-know-whom. This time, the same white District Attorney prosecuted the boy, who was now 17-years old, in front of the black judge Janie Lewis and a mixed but majority-black jury, and the result was quite different. The evidence was overwhelming and not circumstantial. The boy's sperm was found in the girl. He was convicted of first-degree murder, rape, assault and battery, and attempted murder. He was sent to prison for life. Now THAT was justice served.

The irony of this case—and this is where it all hits home for me—the murderer/rapist is the son of my grade-school black friend Roy. He is an illegitimate son, but Roy has never disavowed him. And the mother? Well, she was also a classmate of mine, a black girl named Brenda. Roy was raised in a decent Christian home. Brenda I'm not sure about, but I know I always thought she was a decent person (as were her two brothers as well) all those years that we went to school together. How could she raise such an awful child? I don't know the answer to that. It may or may not be bad parenting that created this monster. I'm sure if you asked a dozen people you'd get a half-dozen different answers.

I feel fortunate to have escaped the gravity of Holmes County back in 1994. Just moving to a small city in Mississippi (Cleveland) with a university (Delta State), be it ever so humble, was a major move up in the world. At least there, I could quench my thirst for knowledge and exercise my intellect through intelligent dialogue and debate with other academics. A couple of my history professors there used to make light of my hailing from Holmes County, proclaiming proudly that they had "rescued" me from its clutches! And so they had.

In 1997, I remarried and moved to Starkville, another small city without much attraction other than the fact that it is home to the largest university in Mississippi (Mississippi State). A land-grant college built on agricultural research and industrial engineering back in the 1880s, Mississippi State quickly grew into a comprehensive state university that competed with Ole Miss (technically the University of Mississippi) in Oxford for students, money from the state legislature, and athletic dominance. Rarely over the last 125 years has it succeeded in any of those ambitions, in all probability because Ole Miss has the state's premier law school, which produces the vast majority of the state's politicians (i.e., "state legislators"), and the state's only medical school, which produces not merely physicians but men and women of socio-economic influence. My state university, on the other hand, has traditionally produced farmers, industrialists, engineers, and architects, who are themselves not without influence, but are no match in a head-to-head competition with lawyers and doctors.

What does all of this have to do with anything? Well, a lot actually. Both schools have histories replete with racially-explosive episodes. Ole Miss is most notorious in history, of course, for its refusal to allow James Meredith, a black Air Force veteran from Attala County, to matriculate there in 1962, despite a federal court order, until the intervention of United States Attorney General Robert F. Kennedy broke the will of the governor of Mississippi, Ross Barnett, to continue his defiance. The subsequent escort of Meredith by federal marshals to the campus resulted in a couple of days and nights of rioting, violence, and vandalism, that ended in multiple deaths and woundings. At about the same time that event was capturing national attention, Mississippi State University was quietly defying a different kind of "court" order–not a judicial court order, but a basketball court order. The school's basketball team was among the best in the nation that year, was ranked number 2 overall at the time, and was in line to compete for the national championship, but did not. Instead, the school forfeited its hoop dreams to avoid playing a team from Texas which had black players. In so doing, it ran against the wave of popular opinion nationwide that had begun to accept racial integration as inevitable in college athletics. After this bigoted incident, it would be decades before the Mississippi State basketball program would recover from that self-inflicted setback and again achieve national prominence.

Such is the legacy of the college that I enrolled in for my doctoral program in history in 1997. It seems, therefore, rather ironic that the field of study that I would enter would be African-American history, and that the field's academic advisor was/is a black man. His name is Professor Jenkins, but I always call(ed) him "Dr. J." He took me in, I think, with full cognizance of the awkwardness of my position of being a poor white southern redneck studying black history. We had a few heart-to-heart talks in my first year so that we could each learn where the other was coming from. We developed a mutual respect for one another, although never the closeness that most of my peers enjoyed with their advisors. I won't automatically attribute that to our color difference, though. There are any number of variables that one must consider in a student-advisor relationship, such as how naturally personable and amicable the individuals are, what kind of chemistry they have with one another, where each makes his/her residence, and how busy they are with family matters and work projects. Anyway, he and I managed to work together closely enough for me to become the first white student in his twenty-years as a faculty advisor to complete my doctorate under his tutelage. The significance of this fact is great, for it shows how far southern society, and particularly race relations in Mississippi, has come in just one generation. Prior to the late 1970s, there were no blacks on faculty in the history department at Mississippi State at all. By 2001, there was not only a twenty-year veteran in place there, but he was guiding a doctoral dissertation for a poor white southern redneck! Add to that the fact that also in 2001, Mississippi State hired another black man–a Nigerian named Godfrey Uzoigwe, who is married to a lily-white Irish woman–to be head of the history department. And the   coup de grace: in 2003, Mississippi State University became the first school in the history of the Southeastern Conference to hire a black football coach, when it secured the services of Sylvester Croom. Those who say times haven't changed simply don't know what they're talking about.

What does the future hold for this poor white southern redneck with a Ph. D.? God only knows for sure. But it looks bright from my vantage point. The future of southern race relations also looks bright to me. The future looks bleak for Holmes County, Mississippi, though, and I'm afraid that unfortunate place will get worse before it gets better. All-in-all, we have come a long way. If progress in the next generation is even half as much as it has been in the generation during which I came of age, we will be all right.

INDEX